Math in Focus™

The Singapore Approach

Extra Practice
3A

Author
Bernice Lau Pui Wah

© 2009 Marshall Cavendish International (Singapore) Private Limited

Published by Marshall Cavendish Education
An imprint of Marshall Cavendish International (Singapore) Private Limited
A member of Times Publishing Limited

Marshall Cavendish International (Singapore) Private Limited
Times Centre, 1 New Industrial Road
Singapore 536196
Tel: +65 6411 0820
Fax: +65 6266 3677
E-mail: fps@sg.marshallcavendish.com
Website: www.marshallcavendish.com/education/sg

Distributed by
Great Source
A division of Houghton Mifflin Harcourt Publishing Company
181 Ballardvale Street
P.O. Box 7050
Wilmington, MA 01887-7050
Tel: 1-800-289-4490
Website: www.greatsource.com

First published 2009

All rights reserved. Permission is hereby granted to teachers to reprint or photocopy in classroom quantities, for use by one teacher and his or her students only, the pages in this work that carry the appropriate copyright notice, provided each copy made shows the copyright notice. Such copies may not be sold, and further distribution is expressly prohibited. Except as authorized above, no part of this publication may be reproduced, stored in a retrieval system or transmitted, in any form or by any means, electronic, mechanical, photocopying, recording or otherwise, without the prior written permission of Marshall Cavendish Education.

Math in Focus™ is a trademark of Times Publishing Limited.

Great Source® is a registered trademark of Houghton Mifflin Harcourt Publishing Company.

Math in Focus Extra Practice 3A
ISBN 978-0-669-01571-3

Printed in Singapore

1 2 3 4 5 6 7 8 MCI 16 15 14 13 12 11 10 09

Contents

CHAPTER 1 — Numbers to 10,000

Lesson 1.1	Counting	1
Lesson 1.2	Place Value	5
Lesson 1.3	Comparing and Ordering Numbers	7

Put on Your Thinking Cap!   13

CHAPTER 2 — Mental Math and Estimation

Lesson 2.1	Mental Addition	15
Lesson 2.2	Mental Subtraction	17
Lesson 2.3	More Mental Addition	19
Lesson 2.4	Rounding Numbers to Estimate	21
Lesson 2.5	Using Front-End Estimation	25

Put on Your Thinking Cap!   29

CHAPTER 3 — Addition up to 10,000

Lesson 3.1	Addition Without Regrouping	31
Lesson 3.2	Addition with Regrouping in Hundreds	33
Lesson 3.3	Addition with Regrouping in Ones, Tens, and Hundreds	35

Put on Your Thinking Cap!   41

CHAPTER 4: Subtraction up to 10,000

Lesson 4.1	Subtraction Without Regrouping	45
Lesson 4.2	Subtraction with Regrouping in Hundreds and Thousands	47
Lesson 4.3	Subtraction with Regrouping in Ones, Tens, Hundreds, and Thousands	49
Lesson 4.4	Subtraction Across Zeros	51

Put on Your Thinking Cap! 57

CHAPTER 5: Using Bar Models: Addition and Subtraction

Lesson 5.1	Real-World Problems: Addition and Subtraction (Part 1)	61
Lesson 5.1	Real-World Problems: Addition and Subtraction (Part 2)	65
Lesson 5.1	Real-World Problems: Addition and Subtraction (Part 3)	67

Put on Your Thinking Cap! 69

Test Prep for Chapters 1 to 5 71

CHAPTER 6: Multiplication Tables of 6, 7, 8, and 9

Lesson 6.1	Multiplication Properties	77
Lesson 6.2	Multiply by 6	79
Lesson 6.3	Multiply by 7	83
Lesson 6.4	Multiply by 8	85
Lesson 6.5	Multiply by 9	87
Lesson 6.6	Division: Finding the Number of Items in Each Group	89
Lesson 6.7	Division: Making Equal Groups	95

Put on Your Thinking Cap! 97

CHAPTER 7 Multiplication

Lesson 7.1	Mental Multiplication	99
Lesson 7.2	Multiplying Without Regrouping	101
Lesson 7.3	Multiplying Ones, Tens, and Hundreds with Regrouping (Part 1)	105
Lesson 7.4	Multiplying Ones, Tens, and Hundreds with Regrouping (Part 2)	109

Put on Your Thinking Cap! 111

CHAPTER 8 Division

Lesson 8.1	Mental Division	113
Lesson 8.2	Quotient and Remainder	115
Lesson 8.3	Odd and Even Numbers	117
Lesson 8.4	Division Without Remainder and Regrouping	119
Lesson 8.5	Division with Regrouping in Tens and Ones	121

Put on Your Thinking Cap! 123

CHAPTER 9 Using Bar Models: Multiplication and Division

Lesson 9.1	Real-World Problems: Multiplication	125
Lesson 9.2	Real-World Problems: Two-step Problems with Multiplication	127
Lesson 9.3	Real-World Problems: Division	129
Lesson 9.4	Real-World Problems: Two-step Problems with Division	131

Put on Your Thinking Cap! 135

Mid-Year Test Prep 139
Answers 153

Introducing Math in Focus™
Extra Practice

Extra Practice 3A and *3B*, written to complement *Math in Focus™: The Singapore Approach* Grade 3, offer further practice very similar to the Practice exercises in the Student Books and Workbooks for on-level students.

Extra Practice provides ample questions to reinforce all the concepts taught, and includes challenging questions in the Put on Your Thinking Cap! pages. These pages provide extra non-routine problem-solving opportunities, strengthening critical thinking skills.

Extra Practice is an excellent option for homework, or may be used in class or after school. It is intended for students who simply need more practice to become confident, or secure students who are aiming for excellence.

Name: _____ Date: _____

 Numbers to 10,000

Lesson 1.1 Counting

Write in standard form.

1. five thousand, five _____

2. three thousand, twenty-nine _____

3. seven thousand, four hundred _____

4. nine thousand, nine hundred, nineteen _____

5. eight thousand, eighty-eight _____

Write the numbers in word form.

6. 6,900

   _____

7. 3,077

   _____

8. 4,621

   _____

9. 2,198

   _____

Extra Practice 3A 1

Fill in the blanks.

Example

Thousands	Hundreds	Tens	Ones

___5___ thousands, ___7___ hundreds ___2___ tens ___9___ ones = 5,729

10.

Thousands	Hundreds	Tens	Ones

_____ thousands, _____ hundreds _____ tens _____ ones = _____

2 Chapter 1 Lesson 1.1

11.

Thousands	**Hundreds**	**Tens**	**Ones**

_____ thousands, _____ hundreds _____ tens _____ ones = _____

Complete each number pattern.

12.   3,665   3,765   3,865   _____   _____   _____

13.   7,523   7,623   7,723   _____   _____   _____

14.   1,798   2,798   _____   _____   _____

15.   4,321   5,321   _____   _____   _____

16.   3,894   3,884   _____   _____   _____

17.   5,762   5,752   _____   _____   _____

18.   8,205   7,205   _____   _____   _____

19.   6,127   5,127   _____   _____   _____

Fill in the missing numbers.

20.   10 more than 8,905 is _____.

21.   100 more than 9,327 is _____.

22.   1,000 more than 7,365 is _____.

23.   10 less than 6,738 is _____.

24.   100 less than 5,861 is _____.

25.   1,000 less than 8,495 is _____.

4   **Chapter 1**   Lesson 1.1

Name: _____ Date: _____

Lesson 1.2   Place Value

Fill in the missing numbers.

1. 7 , 2 5 6

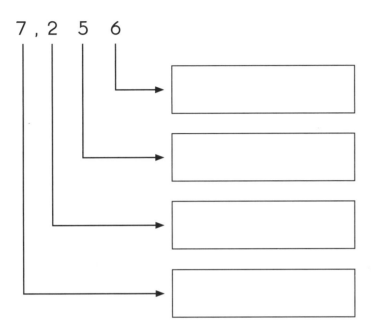

2. In 8,349,

   the digit 3 stands for _____.

   the digit 9 stands for _____.

   the digit 8 stands for _____.

   the digit 4 stands for _____.

Name: _____   Date: _____

Fill in the blanks. Use the place-value chart to help you.

Thousands	Hundreds	Tens	Ones
2	6	9	8

3. In 2,698, the digit 9 is in the _____ place.

   The value of the digit is _____.

4. In 2,698, the digit _____ stands for 600.

   It is in the _____ place.

5. In 2,698, the value of 2 is _____ thousands.

   It is in the _____ place.

6. In 2,698, the digit 8 is in the _____ place.

   It stands for _____.

Fill in the missing numbers.

7. 4,908 = 4,000 + _____ + 8

8. 2,365 = _____ + 300 + 60 + 5

9. 7,068 = 7,000 + 60 + _____

10. _____ = 3,000 + 100 + 90 + 2

11. _____ = 1,000 + 800 + 80 + 9

6 Chapter 1 Lesson 1.2

Lesson 1.3 Comparing and Ordering Numbers

Fill in the blanks.
Use the place-value charts to help you.

1.

Thousands	Hundreds	Tens	Ones
2	7	0	3

_____ is 10 more than 2,703.

2.

Thousands	Hundreds	Tens	Ones
4	5	6	6

_____ is 100 less than 4,666.

Name: _____   Date: _____

3.

Thousands	Hundreds	Tens	Ones

_____ is 1,000 more than 5,256.

Fill in the blanks.

4. _____ is 80 more than 4,020.

5. _____ is 200 more than 8,100.

6. _____ is 4,000 more than 4,875.

7. _____ is 60 less than 8,988.

8. _____ is 100 less than 7,140.

9. _____ is 2,000 less than 9,533.

Name: _____ Date: _____

Fill in the blanks.

10. _____ more than 3,285 is 3,295.

11. _____ more than 3,950 is 4,350.

12. _____ more than 2,854 is 5,854.

13. _____ less than 3,036 is 3,016.

14. _____ less than 7,298 is 7,198.

15. _____ less than 9,382 is 8,382.

Fill in the blanks.

16. 5,555 is _____ more than 5,055.

17. 8,835 is _____ more than 6,835.

18. 9,999 is _____ more than 9,299.

19. 8,904 is _____ less than 9,904.

20. 7,734 is _____ less than 7,834.

21. 4,322 is _____ less than 6,322.

Extra Practice 3A

Name: _____ Date: _____

Circle the greatest number.

22. 2,467   2,476   2,433   2,408

Circle the least number.

23. 8,908   8,900   8,808   8,800

Compare the numbers. Write > or <.

24. 7,733 ◯ 3,377.

25. 3,860 ◯ 3,680.

26. 5,959 ◯ 5,995.

27. 8,063 ◯ 8,073.

Arrange the numbers from greatest to least.

28. 3,572   3,725   3,275   5,237

_____ _____ _____ _____
 greatest

Arrange the numbers from least to greatest.

29. 8,694   8,496   8,964   8,946

_____ _____ _____ _____
 least

Name: _____ Date: _____

Complete each number pattern.

30. 3,465   3,665   3,865   _____   _____

31. 7,839   7,819   _____   _____   7,759

32. 580   2,580   _____   6,580   _____

33. 6,375   6,325   6,275   _____   _____

Fill in the blanks.

34. A watermelon has a mass of 2,360 grams.
    A pumpkin has a mass of 2,630 grams.
    Which fruit is heavier?

    The _____ is heavier than the _____.

35. Container X has 3,590 milliliters of water.
    Container Y has 3,509 milliliters of water.
    Which container has more water?

    Container _____ has more water than Container _____.

Extra Practice 3A   11

Name: _____ **Date:** _____

36. Building A has a height of 1,241 ft.
Building B has a height of 1,214 ft.
Which building is taller?

Building _____ is taller than Building _____.

37. Television set A costs $1,988.
Television set B costs $1,899.
Which television set costs more?

Television set _____ costs more than television set _____.

Name: _____   Date: _____

 **Put on Your Thinking Cap!**

Find the number. Use the clues to help you.

1. Clue 1: It is a 4-digit number.

   Clue 2: The digit in the hundreds place is 5.

   Clue 3: The digit in the tens place is 3 more than the digit in the hundreds place.

   Clue 4: The digit in the ones place is less than 2 but greater than 0.

   Clue 5: The digit in the thousands place is 4 less than the digit in the tens place.

   The number is _____.

Complete each number pattern.

2. 1, 4, 9, 16, 25, _____, _____, _____

3. 100, 200, 400, 700, 1,100, _____, _____, _____

Name: _____   Date: _____

**Form 4-digit numbers. Use the digits given.
Use each digit once only.**

4 7 6 0

4. How many 4-digit numbers can you make?
    _____

5. What is the least 4-digit number you can make?
    _____

6. What is the greatest 4-digit number you can make?
    _____

Circle the mystery number. Use the clues to help you.

7. **118   96   61   47   54**

   Clue 1: The digits in the number add up to a number greater than 10.
   Clue 2: If I count in steps of 2, I will get this number.

   The mystery number is _____.

Name: _____ Date: _____

CHAPTER 2 Mental Math and Estimation

Lesson 2.1 Mental Addition

Fill in the blanks. Use number bonds to help you.

Example

27 + 54 = ?

27 + 50 = __77__

__77__ + __4__ = __81__

So, 27 + 54 = __81__

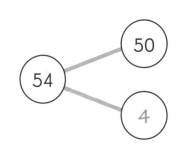

1. 36 + 57 = ?

    36 + 50 = _____

    _____ + _____ = _____

    So, 36 + 57 = _____

    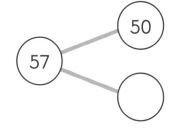

2. 19 + 56 = ?

    19 + 50 = _____

    _____ + _____ = _____

    So, 19 + 56 = _____

    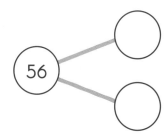

Name: _____ Date: _____

Fill in the blanks. Use number bonds to help you.

--- Example ---
27 + 49 = ?

27 + 50 = __77__

__77__ − __1__ = __76__

So, 27 + 49 = __76__

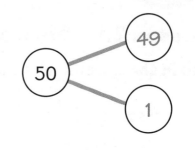

3. 15 + 48 = ?

    15 + 50 = _____

    _____ − _____ = _____

    So, 15 + 48 = _____

4. 26 + 47 = ?

    26 + 50 = _____

    _____ − _____ = _____

    So, 26 + 47 = _____

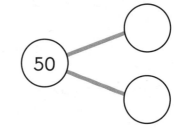

Add. Use mental math.

5. 28 + 56 = _____   6. 34 + 49 = _____

7. 17 + 67 = _____   8. 58 + 47 = _____

9. 55 + 59 = _____   10. 67 + 36 = _____

Name: _____ Date: _____

Lesson 2.2 Mental Subtraction

Fill in the blanks. Use number bonds to help you.

Example

82 − 56 = ?

82 − 50 = __32__

__32__ − __6__ = __26__

So, 82 − 56 = __26__

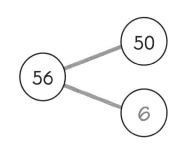

1. 73 − 58 = ?

73 − 50 = _____

_____ − _____ = _____

So, 73 − 58 = _____

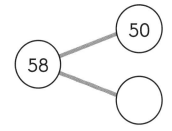

2. 84 − 37 = ?

84 − 30 = _____

_____ − _____ = _____

So, 84 − 37 = _____

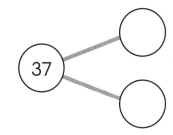

3. 94 − 55 = ?

94 − 50 = _____

_____ − _____ = _____

So, 94 − 55 = _____

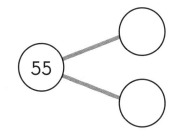

Name: _____ Date: _____

Fill in the blanks. Use number bonds to help you.

— Example —
82 − 18 = ?

82 − 20 = __62__

__62__ + __2__ = __64__

So, 82 − 18 = __64__

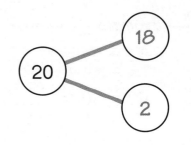

4.   75 − 38 = ?

75 − 40 = _____

_____ + _____ = _____

So, 75 − 38 = _____

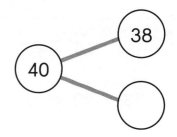

5.   83 − 45 = ?

83 − 50 = _____

_____ + _____ = _____

So, 83 − 45 = _____

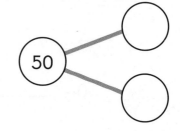

Subtract. Use mental math.

6.   94 − 32 = _____   **7.**   78 − 53 = _____

8.   72 − 25 = _____   **9.**   65 − 38 = _____

10.   51 − 19 = _____   **11.**   84 − 37 = _____

Name: _____   Date: _____

Lesson 2.3 More Mental Addition

Fill in the blanks. Use number bonds to help you.

Example

27 + 97 = ?

27 + 100 = __127__

__127__ − __3__ = __124__

So, 27 + 97 = __124__

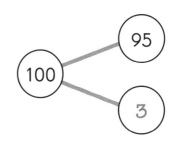

1. 38 + 95 = ?

38 + 100 = _____

_____ − _____ = _____

So, 38 + 95 = _____

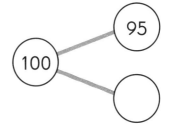

2. 47 + 98 = ?

47 + 100 = _____

_____ − _____ = _____

So, 47 + 98 = _____

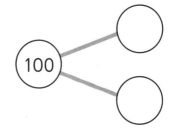

3. 86 + 96 = ?

86 + 100 = _____

_____ − _____ = _____

So, 86 + 96 = _____

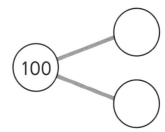

Name: _____ Date: _____

4. 78 + 99 = ?

78 + 100 = _____

_____ − _____ = _____

So, 78 + 99 = _____

5. 66 + 98 = ?

66 + 100 = _____

_____ − _____ = _____

So, 66 + 98 = _____

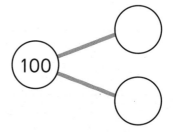

Add. Use mental math.

6. 28 + 96 = _____   **7.** 19 + 94 = _____

8. 47 + 98 = _____   **9.** 69 + 99 = _____

10. 73 + 97 = _____   **11.** 88 + 95 = _____

12. 55 + 96 = _____   **13.** 32 + 99 = _____

14. 44 + 97 = _____   **15.** 78 + 98 = _____

Name: _____   Date: _____

Lesson 2.4   Rounding Numbers to Estimate

Complete the table below.

	Number	Rounded to the nearest	
		tens	hundreds
1.	139		
2.	658		
3.	1,099		
4.	8,567		
5.	4,395		

Round each value to the nearest hundred.

6. A sofa costs $836.

   $836 is $_____ when rounded to the nearest $100.

7. Haven Road is 487 meters long.

   487 meters is _____ meters when rounded to the nearest 100 meter.

8. The distance between two towns is 572 kilometers.

   572 kilometers is _____ kilometers when rounded to the nearest 100 kilometer.

9. A factory can produce 7,970 toys each week.

   7,970 is _____ when rounded to the nearest 100.

Name: _____   Date: _____

Find the greatest and least values for each when rounded to the nearest hundred.

10. A plane flew an estimated distance of 800 kilometers.

    The greatest distance the plane could have flown is _____ kilometers.

    The least distance the plane could have flown is _____ kilometers.

11. A small pool contains about 7,600 liters of water.

    The greatest amount of water the pool could have is _____ liters.

    The least amount of water the pool could have is _____ liters.

Solve. Show your work.

12. Mr. Thomas has $2,000.

    The computer costs about $_____.

    The printer costs about $_____.

    The camera costs about $_____.

    Does Mr. Thomas have enough money to pay for all the items?

    _____

22   Chapter 2   Lesson 2.4

Name: _____ **Date:** _____

● **Find the sum. Use rounding to check that each answer is reasonable.**

> *Example*
>
> 225 + 472 = __697__
>
> 225 is about __200__.
>
> 472 is about __500__.
>
> __200__ + __500__ = __700__
>
> So, 225 + 472 is about __700__.
>
> __697__ is close to __700__, so the answer is reasonable.

● **13.** 780 + 230 = _____

780 is about _____.

230 is about _____.

_____ + _____ = _____

So, 780 + 230 is about _____.

_____ is close to _____, so the answer is reasonable.

Name: _____   Date: _____

14. 748 − 319 = _____

748 is about _____.

319 is about _____.

_____ + _____ = _____

So, 748 + 319 is about _____.

_____ is close to _____, so the answer is reasonable.

15. 527 − 288 = _____

527 is about _____.

288 is about _____.

_____ − _____ = _____

So, 527 − 288 is about _____.

_____ is close to _____, so the answer is reasonable.

Lesson 2.5 Using Front-End Estimation

Find the sum. Use front-end estimation to check that each answer is reasonable.

> **Example**
>
> 219 + 567 = __786__
>
> __200__ + __500__ = __700__
>
> The estimated sum is __700__.
>
> The answer __786__ is reasonable.

1. 268 + 323 = _____

_____ + _____ = _____

The estimated sum is _____.

The answer _____ is reasonable.

2. 479 + 624 = _____

_____ + _____ = _____

The estimated sum is _____.

The answer _____ is reasonable.

Extra Practice 3A **25**

Name: _____ Date: _____

Find the difference. Use front-end estimation to check that each answer is reasonable.

3.   574 − 296 = _____

   _____ − _____ = _____

   The estimated difference is _____.

   Is the answer reasonable? _____.

4.   916 − 378 = _____

   _____ − _____ = _____

   The estimated difference is _____.

   Is the answer reasonable? _____.

Find the sum or difference. Use front-end estimation to check that each answer is reasonable.

5.   260 + 350 = _____

   _____ + _____ = _____

   The estimated sum is _____.

   Is the answer reasonable? _____.

6.   425 + 272 = _____

   _____ + _____ = _____

   The estimated sum is _____.

   Is the answer reasonable? _____.

26   Chapter 2   Lesson 2.5

Name: _____ Date: _____

7. 590 − 466 = _____

_____ − _____ = _____

The estimated difference is _____.

Is the answer reasonable? _____.

8. 780 − 690 = _____

_____ − _____ = _____

The estimated difference is _____.

Is the answer reasonable? _____.

Solve. Show your work.

9. Beatrice has 136 books.
Her brother has twice as many books as Beatrice.
Estimate the number of books they have altogether.

10. A grocer sells 548 apples and 470 oranges.
Estimate the number of fruit he sells altogether.

11. Kathy and Joe go for a jog.
Kathy jogs 650 meters and Joe jogs 480 meters.
Estimate the difference in the distances that they jog.

Name: _____   Date: _____

 # Put on Your Thinking Cap!

Add or subtract mentally.
Fill in the missing numbers in the puzzle.

1.

134	+	53	=	
−				
56				
=				
	+	47	=	
				−
				49
				=
22	+		=	

Add or subtract mentally.

2. 394 + 98 = _____   3. 206 + 103 = _____

4. 445 − 99 = _____   5. 788 − 106 = _____

6. 237 + 97 = _____   7. 313 − 109 = _____

Name: _____ Date: _____

Shade the given numbers. Then, fill in the next three numbers.

Example

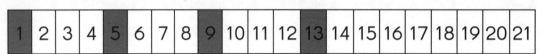

1, 5, 9, __13__, __17__, __21__

8.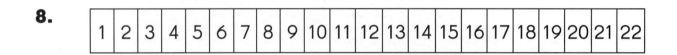

1, 2, 4, 7, _____, _____, _____

Complete each number pattern.

9.   1, 2, 5, 10, 17, _____, _____, _____

10. 1, 2, 4, 8, 16, _____, _____, _____

Name: _____   Date: _____

 **Addition up to 10,000**

Lesson 3.1 Addition Without Regrouping

Add. Use a place-value chart to help you.

1.

Thousands	Hundreds	Tens	Ones
4	3	5	6
+	6	4	3

2.

Thousands	Hundreds	Tens	Ones
2	4	1	7
+	3	6	2

3.

Thousands	Hundreds	Tens	Ones
3	5	2	3
+ 4	3	7	3

4.

Thousands	Hundreds	Tens	Ones
5	1	2	4
+ 3	6	7	4

Extra Practice 3A 31

Name: _____   Date: _____

Add.

5.   1, 4 3 2
   + 2, 3 1 4
   ☐

6.   3, 4 2 6
   + 1, 2 5 2
   ☐

7.   2, 5 3 4
   + 3, 0 2 4
   ☐

8.   4, 6 2 7
   + 1, 2 4 2
   ☐

9.   5, 8 3 7
   + 2, 1 5 2
   ☐

10. 3, 4 2 6
   + 1, 2 5 2
   ☐

Add.

11. 6,083 + 2,003 = _____

12. 7,500 + 437 = _____

13. 2,404 + 3,000 = _____

14. 5,025 + 3,114 = _____

15. 7,612 + 2,212 = _____

16. 4,236 + 2,600 = _____

Name: _____ Date: _____

Lesson 3.2 Addition with Regrouping in Hundreds

Find the missing numbers.

1. 4 hundreds + 8 hundreds

   = _____ hundreds

   = _____ thousand _____ hundreds

2. 6 hundreds + 8 hundreds

   = _____ hundreds

   = _____ thousand _____ hundreds

3. 7 hundreds + 9 hundreds

   = _____ hundreds

   = _____ thousand _____ hundreds

4. 9 hundreds + 9 hundreds

   = _____ hundreds

   = _____ thousand _____ hundreds

5. 8 hundreds + 5 hundreds

   = _____ hundreds

   = _____ thousand _____ hundreds

Extra Practice 3A

Name: _____   Date: _____

Add.

6.   2, 6 5 9
    +   8 0 0
   ☐

7.   3, 4 0 6
    +   7 1 3
   ☐

8.   4, 5 4 2
    + 2, 9 2 3
   ☐

9.   5, 6 1 5
    + 3, 6 0 4
   ☐

10.   6, 7 2 9
    + 1, 8 3 0
   ☐

11.   5, 8 0 7
    + 3, 9 8 2
   ☐

Add.

12. The sum of 3,684 and 2,700 is ☐ .

13. The sum of 3,503 and 5,956 is ☐ .

14. 5,833 + 3,465 = ☐

15. 7,944 + 1,845 = ☐

Lesson 3.3 Addition with Regrouping in Ones, Tens, and Hundreds

Add.

1.
```
   7 3 8
+  6 9 5
--------
```

2.
```
   8 6 7
+  3 6 7
--------
```

3.
```
   6 7 9
+  8 4 6
--------
```

4.
```
   5 6 7
+  9 4 8
--------
```

5.
```
   2, 9 4 6
+  3, 6 8 8
----------
```

6.
```
   3, 7 5 2
+  3, 5 6 8
----------
```

7.
```
   4, 2 7 6
+  4, 7 8 9
----------
```

8.
```
   1, 8 1 9
+  6, 3 9 9
----------
```

Name: _____ Date: _____

9.   6, 4 8 5
 + 2, 6 8 8

10.   5, 2 4 6
 + 3, 9 7 8

11.   3, 7 2 9
 + 2, 6 8 4

12.   4, 2 5 3
 + 1, 9 5 9

13.   4, 5 7 6
 + 3, 8 7 9

14.   6, 8 5 6
 + 1, 4 5 6

15.   7, 3 9 4
 + 1, 8 3 8

16.   3, 9 9 5
 + 2, 6 4 7

17.   2, 5 4 9
 + 5, 6 6 2

18.   1, 1 8 3
 + 3, 9 2 7

Name: _____ Date: _____

Solve. Show your work.

19. Durai bought a computer for $1,346.
He bought a printer for $452.
How much did Durai pay in all?

20. At Hillside Elementary School, there are 1,253 boys
and 1,624 girls.
How many students are there at the school?

Name: _____ Date: _____

21. Mr. Li has 1,034 goats.
He has 242 more sheep than goats.
How many sheep does Mr. Li have?

22. Mr. George spent $1,008 on a couch.
He spent $1,860 more on a plasma TV than he did on the couch.
How much did Mr. George spend on the plasma TV?

23. The Boy Scouts collected 2,486 gifts for a children's home.
The Girl Scouts collected 3,787 gifts for a senior center.
How many gifts did they collect in all?

24. In a library, there are 4,767 English books and 4,594 French books.
How many books does the library have in all?

25. At a farm, there are 256 chickens and 4,857 ducks.
How many chickens and ducks are there at the farm altogether?

26. A baker baked 1,464 rolls on Saturday.
He baked 1,867 more rolls on Sunday than on Saturday.
How many rolls did he bake on Sunday?

Name: _____   Date: _____

 **Put on Your Thinking Cap!**

Find the mystery numbers.

1. The sum of two numbers is 200.
   One number is 40 less than the other number.

   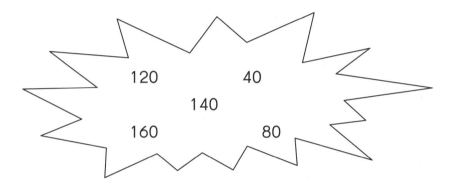

   The numbers are _____ and _____.

2. The sum of two numbers is 190.
   The sum of their digits is 10.

   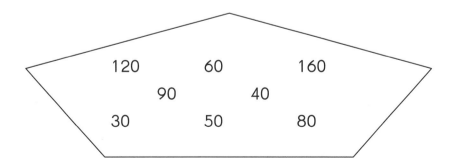

   The numbers are _____ and _____.

Extra Practice 3A   41

Name: _____ Date: _____

3. **Place the following digits in the boxes so that the sum of the digits in each straight line is the same.**

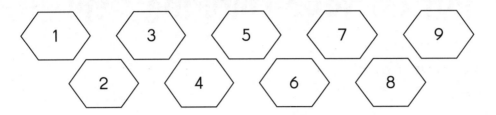

There is more than one possible answer.

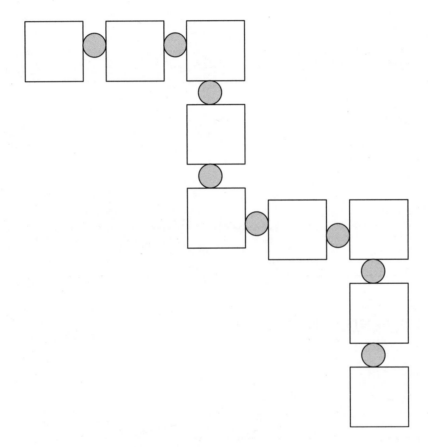

42 Chapter 3 Put on Your Thinking Cap!

4. **Use the following digits to form 4-digit numbers.**

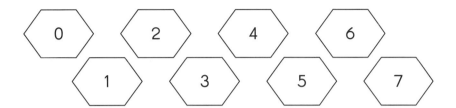

Use each digit only once. Do not begin a number with the digit 0.

Form the smallest sum of two 4-digit numbers.

a.

Form the greatest sum of two 4-digit numbers.
The sum must be less than 10,000.

b.

Extra Practice 3A   43

Name: _____   Date: _____

5. **John thinks of a 3-digit number.
What is his number?
Use the clues below to find John's number.**

> Every digit is different.
> The sum of all the digits is 19.
> The difference between the hundreds digit and the ones digit is 6.
> The tens digit is the greatest digit.
> The number is greater than 500.

John's number is _____.

Name: _____ Date: _____

 Subtraction up to 10,000

Lesson 4.1 Subtraction Without Regrouping

Subtract. Use a place-value chart to help you.

1.

Thousands	Hundreds	Tens	Ones
2	7	6	6
−	4	4	5

2.

Thousands	Hundreds	Tens	Ones
6	9	8	4
−	6	3	2

3.

Thousands	Hundreds	Tens	Ones
5	4	7	9
− 2	0	3	5

4.

Thousands	Hundreds	Tens	Ones
6	5	8	7
− 4	3	4	3

Extra Practice 3A

Name: _____   Date: _____

Subtract.

5.   7, 8 2 5
   − 2, 2 0 4
   ☐

6.   8, 0 4 3
   − 4, 0 1 2
   ☐

7.   6, 3 7 2
   − 3, 2 6 0
   ☐

8.   9, 9 5 8
   − 6, 4 3 5
   ☐

Circle the two numbers that give the difference. Then write the number sentence.

9. The difference between the numbers is 230.

   420   379   178   650

10. The difference between the numbers is 325.

   900   145   575   165

46 Chapter 4 Lesson 4.1

Name: _____ Date: _____

Lesson 4.2 Subtraction with Regrouping in Hundreds and Thousands

Find the missing numbers.

> *Example*
> 3 thousands 5 hundreds
> = 2 thousands ___15___ hundreds.

1. 4 thousands 6 hundreds

   = 3 thousands _____ hundreds.

2. 8 thousands 3 hundreds

   = 7 thousands _____ hundreds.

3. 5 thousands 8 hundreds

   = 4 thousands _____ hundreds.

4. 9 thousands 7 hundreds

   = 8 thousands _____ hundreds.

5. 7 thousands 2 hundreds

   = 6 thousands _____ hundreds.

Name: _____   Date: _____

Subtract. Use a place-value chart to help you.

6.

Thousands	Hundreds	Tens	Ones
4	3	6	0
− 2	5	4	0

7.

Thousands	Hundreds	Tens	Ones
5	4	3	6
− 1	7	2	3

8.

Thousands	Hundreds	Tens	Ones
8	0	6	7
− 4	6	2	5

9.

Thousands	Hundreds	Tens	Ones
7	5	9	6
− 6	7	8	6

Name: _____ Date: _____

Lesson 4.3   Subtraction with Regrouping in Ones, Tens, Hundreds, and Thousands

Regroup. Find the missing numbers.

1. 6 hundreds 2 tens = 5 hundreds [   ] tens

2. 3 hundreds 5 tens = 2 hundreds [   ] tens

3. 8 hundreds 3 tens = 7 hundreds [   ] tens

4. 7 tens 4 ones = 6 tens [   ] ones

5. 3 tens 6 ones = 2 tens [   ] ones

6. 8 tens 9 ones = 7 tens [   ] ones

Subtract. Regroup when needed.

7.

Thousands	Hundreds	Tens	Ones
5	3	1	0
− 3	5	4	6

8.

Thousands	Hundreds	Tens	Ones
8	2	2	3
− 3	4	3	9

Extra Practice 3A   **49**

Name: _____ Date: _____

9.

Thousands	Hundreds	Tens	Ones
6	4	1	8
− 3	7	2	9

10.

Thousands	Hundreds	Tens	Ones
7	0	4	6
− 1	6	5	8

11.

Thousands	Hundreds	Tens	Ones
7	2	0	3
− 2	7	8	5

12.

Thousands	Hundreds	Tens	Ones
9	3	2	4
− 5	5	6	6

13.

Thousands	Hundreds	Tens	Ones
8	1	3	5
− 6	4	8	7

Chapter 4 Lesson 4.3

Name: _____ Date: _____

Lesson 4.4 Subtraction Across Zeros

Subtract. Use a place-value chart to help you.

1.

	Thousands	Hundreds	Tens	Ones
	1	0	0	0
−		3	2	0

2.

	Thousands	Hundreds	Tens	Ones
	2	0	0	0
−	1	0	2	0

3.

	Thousands	Hundreds	Tens	Ones
	8	0	0	5
−	3	2	4	6

4.

	Thousands	Hundreds	Tens	Ones
	7	0	1	0
−	5	8	4	5

Extra Practice 3A

Subtract. Then solve.

5.
```
  1, 0 0 0
-    4 8 0
```
(P)

6.
```
  3, 0 0 0
- 1, 2 5 4
```
(I)

7.
```
  5, 0 0 0
- 2, 5 8 6
```
(R)

8.
```
  6, 0 0 0
- 2, 9 3 6
```
(C)

9.
```
  7, 0 0 5
- 3, 4 6 8
```
(F)

10.
```
  8, 0 6 0
- 2, 3 8 4
```
(U)

11.
```
  5, 2 0 0
- 4, 8 3 7
```
(A)

12.
```
  9, 0 1 0
- 5, 1 9 2
```
(O)

Name: _____   Date: _____

13.

```
   1, 0 0 0
 -    7 2 6
```
[N _____]

Help Jenny solve the riddle.
Write the corresponding letters to find out.

What kind of pine has the sharpest needles?

_____ _____ _____ _____
 (363)   (520)   (3,818) (2,414)

_____ _____ _____ _____
(3,064) (5,676)   (520)   (1,746)

_____ _____
 (274)   (3,537)

Solve. Show your work.

14. Mrs. Jones has 726 pencils.
She wants to give 4,005 children one pencil each.
How many more pencils does Mrs. Jones need?

Extra Practice 3A   53

Name: _____ Date: _____

15. Lena had $2,050.
She buys a computer for $1,598.
How much money does Lena have left?

16. A farmer has 3,670 sheep on his farm.
There are 1,982 fewer cows than sheep on the farm.
How many cows are there?

Name: _____   Date: _____

17. Mr. Rajan earns $3,000 a month.
He spends $1,346 a month and saves the rest.
How much money does Mr. Rajan save each month?

18. At ABC gas station, 2,570 liters of gasoline are sold on Monday, and 5,870 liters of gasoline are sold on Tuesday. Find the difference between the amounts of gasoline sold on the two days.

Extra Practice 3A   55

Name: _____ Date: _____

19. A performance was attended by 3,058 adults and 1,735 children. How many fewer children than adults were at the performance?

20. Mr. Bema needs exactly 1,260 kilograms of flour for his factory. He has 985 kilograms of flour now. How many more kilograms of flour does Mr. Bema need?

Name: _____   Date: _____

 **Put on Your Thinking Cap!**

1. Tran is thinking of two 3-digit numbers.
   Use the clues below to find Tran's numbers.

   > The sum of these two numbers is 500.
   > The difference between these two numbers is 220.
   > The smaller number is less than 200.
   > The greater number is more than 300.

   What are the two 3-digit numbers?

   The numbers are _____ and _____.

   Extra Practice 3A   **57**

Name: _____ Date: _____

2. **Use the following digits to form 4-digit numbers.**

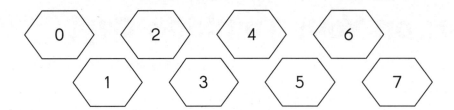

Use each digit only once.
Do not begin a number with the digit 0.

a. Form the greatest difference of two 4-digit numbers.

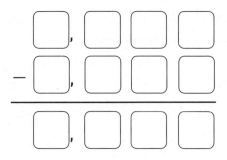

b. Form the smallest difference of two 4-digit numbers.

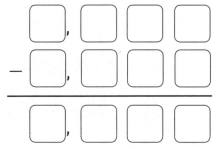

3. Sondhi, Larry, and Moe are at a carnival stall. Each of them has 3 balls to throw at the targets.

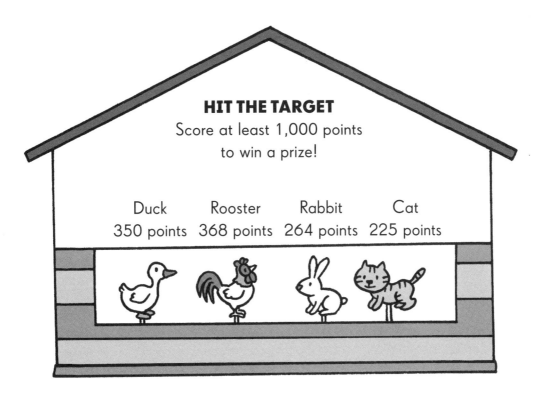

HIT THE TARGET
Score at least 1,000 points to win a prize!

Duck 350 points Rooster 368 points Rabbit 264 points Cat 225 points

a. Sondhi hits 1 cat and 2 roosters.
Larry hits 1 duck and 2 rabbits.
Who scores more points?
Does he win a prize?

b. Moe has a total of 1,000 points.
What targets did he hit?

Name: _____ Date: _____

4. Hassan has four cards. Each card has a number on it as shown below.

a. Form 4-digit numbers by using each card only once.
List the four-digit numbers that are greater than 7,000.

b. Find the difference between the greatest and least 4-digit numbers from the above list.

Name: _____ Date: _____

Using Bar Models: Addition and Subtraction

Lesson 5.1 Real-World Problems: Addition and Subtraction (Part 1)

Solve. Draw bar models to help you.

1. Mrs. Tan buys a duck and a chicken.
The mass of the duck is 2,300 grams.
The mass of the chicken is 1,675 grams.
How much heavier is the duck than the chicken?

2. Allison jogs 3,860 meters and Calvin jogs 5,470 meters.
How far do they jog altogether?

Extra Practice 3A **61**

Name: _____ Date: _____

3. John and Tracy sell flags to raise money for their club. John sells 457 flags and Tracy sells 686 flags.

    a. How many flags do they sell in all?

    b. Who sells more flags? How many more?

4. On Valentine's Day, Kiri makes 96 bookmarks. Zelda makes 120 bookmarks.

    a. How many more bookmarks does Zelda make than Kiri?

    b. How many bookmarks do they make altogether?

5. Leila drinks 1,466 milliliters of water a day.
Mark drinks 2,895 milliliters more than Leila.

a. How much water does Mark drink?

b. How much water do they drink in all?

6. Brad has 1,300 stamps.
He has 938 Canadian stamps and the rest are Malaysian stamps.

a. How many Malaysian stamps does Brad have?

b. Which type of stamps does Brad have fewer of?
How many fewer stamps?

7. Minah buys a sofa and a dining set for her new apartment.

Sofa

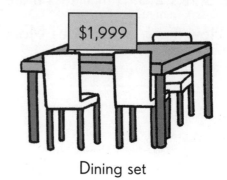
Dining set

a. Which item is less expensive?

b. How much less expensive is it?

Lesson 5.1 Real-World Problems: Addition and Subtraction (Part 2)

Solve. Draw bar models to help you.

1. A computer costs $1,590.
   A printer costs $899.

   a. How much less expensive is the printer than the computer?

   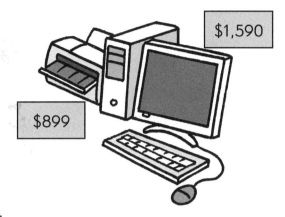

   b. How much do the two items cost altogether?

2. There are 3,160 books and magazines in a shop. There are 2,378 books. The rest are magazines.

   a. How many magazines are there?

   b. There are 1,226 English books in the shop and the rest are French books. How many French books are there?

Extra Practice 3A   65

Name: _____ **Date:** _____

3. Mr. Michael has $1,685.
Ms. Katty has $2,928 more than Mr. Michael.

   a. How much money does Ms. Katty have?

   b. How much money do they have in all?

4. There are 3,254 children at a concert.
There are 1,369 fewer adults than children attending the concert.

   a. How many adults are there at the concert?

   b. How many people are at the concert altogether?

Name: _____ Date: _____

Lesson 5.1 Real-World Problems: Addition and Subtraction (Part 3)

Solve. Draw bar models to help you.

1. The pictures below show the number of marbles in each bag.

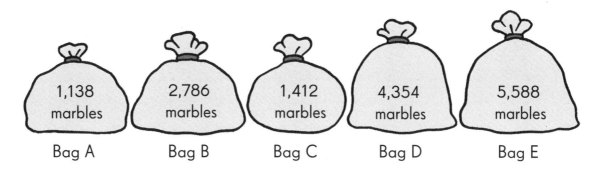

Bag A: 1,138 marbles
Bag B: 2,786 marbles
Bag C: 1,412 marbles
Bag D: 4,354 marbles
Bag E: 5,588 marbles

Jane takes Bag B and Bag D.
Karen takes Bag E.

a. Who has more marbles?

b. How many more marbles does she have?

Extra Practice 3A **67**

2. In Green Bridge Elementary School, there are 159 adults, 1,960 boys, and 558 fewer girls than boys. How many people are there in the school?

3. Ravi has 1,286 stamps. Terell has 1,528 more stamps than Ravi. How many stamps do they have in all?

Name: _____   Date: _____

 **Put on Your Thinking Cap!**

1. Place the following digits in the boxes so that the sum of the 3-digit numbers is 999. Use each digit only once.

   ① ② ③ ④ ⑤ ⑥ ⑦ ⑧ ⑨

   ```
       ☐ ☐ ☐
       ☐ ☐ ☐
   +   ☐ ☐ ☐
   ───────────
       9 9 9
   ```

2. Teresa has 300 red and green apples.
   There are 40 more red apples than green apples.
   How many green apples does Teresa have?

Extra Practice 3A   **69**

3. Tashi thinks of a 4-digit number.
What is her number?
Use the clues below to find Tashi's number.

> Every digit is different.
> The sum of the thousands digit and the tens digit is 10.
> The sum of all the digits is 16.
> The difference between the hundreds digit and the ones digit is 6.
> The difference between the thousands digit and the hundreds digit is 3.
> The number is greater than 8,000.

Tashi's number is _____.

Name: _____   Date: _____

Test Prep
for Chapters 1 to 5

/50

Multiple Choice (10 × 2 points = 20 points)

Fill in the circle next to the correct answer.

1. In the number 7,348, the digit 7 is in the ☐ place.

   Ⓐ ones   Ⓑ tens   Ⓒ hundreds   Ⓓ thousands

2. How many hundreds are there in the number 3,628?

   Ⓐ 6   Ⓑ 36   Ⓒ 62   Ⓓ 600

3. In the number pattern, what is the missing number?

   3,888, 4,438, 5,088, 5,838, ☐

   Ⓐ 6,088   Ⓑ 6,288   Ⓒ 6,488   Ⓓ 6,688

4. Subtract 3,854 from 10,000. The answer is ☐.

   Ⓐ 6,146   Ⓑ 6,246   Ⓒ 7,146   Ⓓ 7,246

5. Add 2,659 to 784. The sum is ☐ more than 555.

   Ⓐ 2,878   Ⓑ 2,888   Ⓒ 2,988   Ⓓ 3,988

Extra Practice 3A   71

Name: _____ Date: _____

6. 45 + 5 = ☐ − 100. The missing number is _____.

  Ⓐ 30   Ⓑ 70   Ⓒ 130   Ⓓ 170

7. Add 567 to the difference of 8,000 and 4,567.

  The answer is ☐.

  Ⓐ 2,866   Ⓑ 3,866   Ⓒ 4,000   Ⓓ 6,000

8. Liling bought a toy for $28.
  She paid $19 more for a model car than she paid for the toy.
  How much did Liling pay in all?

  Ⓐ $47   Ⓑ $57   Ⓒ $65   Ⓓ $75

9. Mr. King has 3,120 fish in his aquarium.
  After he sells 1,850 fish, how many fish does Mr. King have left?

  Ⓐ 1,250   Ⓑ 1,270   Ⓒ 1,370   Ⓓ 2,270

10. Banner A is 385 centimeters long.
  Banner B is 169 centimeters longer than Banner A.
  What is the total length of the two banners?

  Ⓐ 554 cm   Ⓑ 839 cm   Ⓒ 854 cm   Ⓓ 939 cm

Name: _____ Date: _____

Short Answer (10 × 2 points = 20 points)

Write your answers in the space given.

11. Write 6,999 in word form.

    Answer: _____

12. In the number 8,296, what is the value of the digit 2?

    Answer: _____

13. In the number 3,749, the digit 4 is in the ☐ place.

    Answer: _____

14. What number is 500 less than 6,125?

    Answer: _____

15. What is the smallest 4-digit number that can be formed with the digits 3, 8, 0, and 7?

    Answer: _____

16. Subtract 989 from the sum of 1,857 and 2,465.

    Answer: _____

17. Complete the number pattern.

Answer: _____

18. Lena has 258 coins.
Shanta has 75 more coins than Lena.
How many coins does Shanta have?

Answer: _____ coins

19. Nordin has 523 marbles.
He has 68 more marbles than Vivian.
How many marbles does Vivian have?

Answer: _____ marbles

20. I am a 3-digit number that is less than 500.
My ones digit is twice the hundreds digit.
The sum of the three digits is 14.
What number am I?

Answer: _____

Name: _____ Date: _____

Extended Response (10 points)

Solve. Show your work.

21. Meena, Fiona, and Jacob share a total of 320 seashells.
    Fiona gets 140 seashells.
    Meena gets 90 seashells.
    How many seashells does Jacob get?
    (2 points)

Draw a model to help you.

22. Kerrie has 100 American and Danish stamps.
    She has 60 more American stamps than Danish stamps.
    How many Danish stamps does Kerrie have?
    (3 points)

Extra Practice 3A

Name: _____ Date: _____

23. Latoya has 75 fewer cards than Andrew.
Clinton has 38 more cards than Latoya.
Clinton has 200 cards. How many picture cards does
Andrew have? (3 points)

Draw a model to help you.

24. Look at the numbers below.

   5,726   5,672

   a. How are these two numbers similar? (1 point)

   _____

   b. How are these two numbers different? (1 point)

   _____

Name: _____   Date: _____

Multiplication Tables of 6, 7, 8, and 9

Lesson 6.1   Multiplication Properties

Look at each number line. Write the multiplication fact.

1.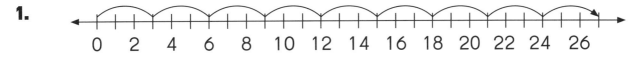

   _____ × _____ = _____

2.

   _____ × _____ = _____

3.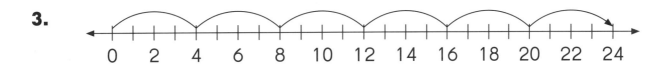

   _____ × _____ = _____

4.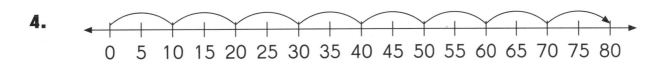

   _____ × _____ = _____

Extra Practice 3A   77

Name: _____ Date: _____

Multiply. Use skip counting to help you.

5. 8 × 2 = _____   6. 4 × 4 = _____

7. 5 × 0 = _____   8. 6 × 3 = _____

9. 7 × 4 = _____   10. 8 × 5 = _____

11. 6 × 10 = _____   12. 7 × 3 = _____

Fill in the missing numbers.

13. 4 × _____ = _____ × 4 = 20

14. _____ × 3 = 3 × _____ = 24

15. 10 × _____ = _____ × 10 = 90

16. _____ × 5 = 5 × _____ = 45

17. _____ × 2 = 16

18. _____ × 3 = 27

19. 4 × _____ = 36

20. 5 × _____ = 25

Name: _____   Date: _____

Lesson 6.2   Multiply by 6

Look at each array model. Then fill in the blanks.

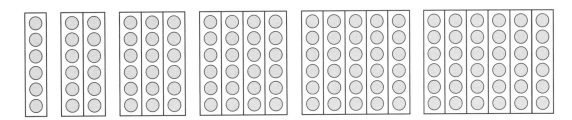

1. a. 6   12   _____   24   _____   36

    b. 30   36   42   _____   _____   _____

Fill in the missing numbers.

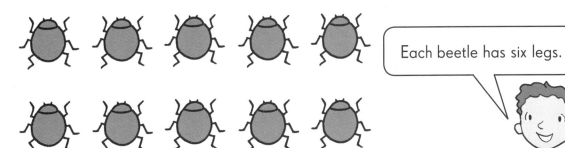

Each beetle has six legs.

2. a. 2 × 6 = _____

    b. 4 × 6 = _____

    c. 6 × 6 = _____

    d. 8 × 6 = _____

    e. _____ × 6 = 18

    f. _____ × 6 = 42

    g. 9 × 6 = 6 × _____ = _____

    h. 10 × _____ = _____ × 10 = 60

Extra Practice 3A   **79**

Name: _____ Date: _____

Multiply. Use related multiplication facts to help you.

3. a. 6 + 6 + 6 + 6 + 6 = _____ × 6

   b.
   $\left. \begin{array}{l} \bigcirc\bigcirc\bigcirc\bigcirc\bigcirc\bigcirc \\ \bigcirc\bigcirc\bigcirc\bigcirc\bigcirc\bigcirc \\ \bigcirc\bigcirc\bigcirc\bigcirc\bigcirc\bigcirc \\ \bigcirc\bigcirc\bigcirc\bigcirc\bigcirc\bigcirc \\ \bigcirc\bigcirc\bigcirc\bigcirc\bigcirc\bigcirc \end{array} \right\} 5 \times 6 = 30$

   $\left. \begin{array}{l} \bullet\bullet\bullet\bullet\bullet\bullet \\ \bullet\bullet\bullet\bullet\bullet\bullet \end{array} \right\} 2 \times 6 = 12$

   $\Big\} 7 \times 6 = $ _____

   7 × 6 = 5 × 6 + _____ × 6

   c. 12 = _____ × 6

   24 = _____ × 6

   12 + 24 = _____ × 6 + _____ × 6

   = _____ × 6

   = _____

   d. 18 = _____ × 6

   36 = _____ × 6

   54 = _____ × 6 + 6 × 6

Name: _____   Date: _____

Solve. Show your work.

4. Pencils are given to 4 children.
    Each child has 6 pencils.
    How many pencils do the children have in all?

5. A pet store owner keeps 6 birds in each cage.
    How many birds does he keep in 8 cages?

Extra Practice 3A   81

Name: _____ Date: _____

6. Jason makes 6 bookmarks in an hour.
How many bookmarks can he make in 7 hours?

7. Siti has 9 dolls.
Each doll costs $6.
How much do the 9 dolls cost in all?

Name: _____ Date: _____

Lesson 6.3 Multiply by 7

Look at each area model. Write the multiplication fact.

1.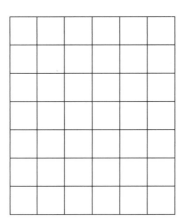

   _____ × _____ = _____

2.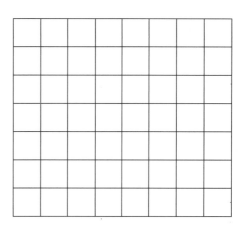

   _____ × _____ = _____

Fill in the missing numbers.

3. 2 × 7 = _____   4. 4 × 7 = _____

5. 5 × 7 = _____   6. 8 × 7 = _____

7. 7 × _____ = 49   8. _____ × 7 = 63

9. _____ × 7 = 7 × _____ = 21

10. _____ × 7 = 7 × _____ = 0

Extra Practice 3A

Name: _____ Date: _____

Fill in the missing numbers.

11.   8 × 7 = 4 × 7 + _____ × 7

12.   6 × 7 = 3 × 7 + _____ × 7

Solve. Show your work.

13.   For a relay race, teams of 7 children each are formed. How many children are there in 6 teams?

14.   When 36 is added to a number, the answer is the same as multiplying the number by 7.
What is the number?

Name: _____ Date: _____

Lesson 6.4 Multiply by 8

Complete each skip-counting pattern.

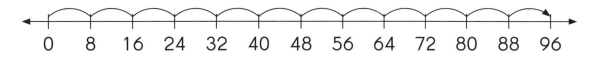

1. 8   16   _____   _____   _____   48

2. 40   _____   _____   _____   72   _____

Fill in the missing numbers.

3.

I have 8 tentacles.

×	1	3	5	9	8	7	4	6	10
8	8	24							

Fill in the missing numbers.

4. 2 × 8 = _____ × 2 = _____

5. 8 + 8 + 8 + 8 + 24 = _____ × 8

6. 40 = _____ × 8 = 8 × _____

7. 40 + 40 = _____ × 8 + _____ × 8

         = _____

Extra Practice 3A   **85**

Solve. Show your work.

8. Keenan spends $8 a day.
    How much does he spend in a week?

Monday	$8
Tuesday	$8
Wednesday	$8
Thursday	$8
Friday	$8
Saturday	$8
Sunday	$8

9. Mrs. Li has 9 grandchildren.
    She gives each grandchild 8 storybooks.
    How many storybooks does Mrs. Li give altogether?

Lesson 6.5 Multiply by 9

Fill in the missing numbers.

1.

"I am holding up 9 fingers."

×	1	3	5	9	8	7	4	6	10
9	9	27							

Multiply. Use related multiplication facts to help you.

2. 9×9 = 5 groups of 9 + _____ groups of 9

   = _____ + _____

   = _____

   OR

   9×9 = 10 groups of 9 − _____ group of 9

   = _____ − _____

   = _____

Name: _____ Date: _____

Solve. Show your work.

3. Pam buys 9 cartons of milk.
She pays $4 for each carton.
How much does Pam pay in all?

4. When 56 is added to a number, the answer is the same as multiplying the number by 9.
What is the number?

Name: _____ Date: _____

Lesson 6.6 Division: Finding the Number of Items in Each Group

**Circle to make equal groups.
Then fill in the missing numbers.**

1.

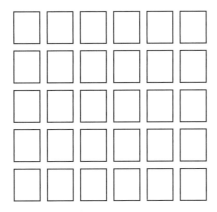

30 ÷ 5 = _____
Each group has

_____ squares.

2.

48 ÷ 6 = _____
Each group has

_____ hearts.

3.

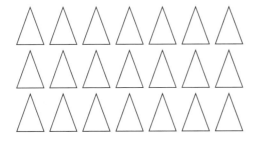

21 ÷ 3 = _____
Each group has

_____ triangles.

4.

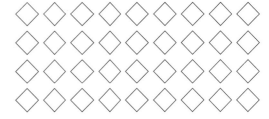

36 ÷ 4 = _____
Each group has

_____ diamonds.

Extra Practice 3A

Name: _____ Date: _____

Fill in the missing numbers.

5. 7 × _____ = 56   So, 56 ÷ 7 = _____

6. 8 × _____ = 72   So, 72 ÷ 8 = _____

7. 9 × _____ = 54   So, 54 ÷ 9 = _____

8. 6 × _____ = 42   So, 42 ÷ 6 = _____

**Each square is the product of the circles on either side of it.
Fill in the missing numbers.
Then use each multiplication fact to write two division facts.**

Example

_4_ × _7_ = _28_

_28_ ÷ _4_ = _7_

_28_ ÷ _7_ = _4_

_8_ × _7_ = _56_

_56_ ÷ _7_ = _8_

_56_ ÷ _8_ = _7_

_4_ × _8_ = _32_

_32_ ÷ _4_ = _8_

_32_ ÷ _8_ = _4_

90 Chapter 6 Lesson 6.6

Name: _____ **Date:** _____

9.

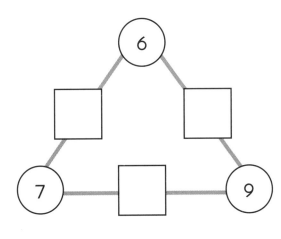

_____ × _____ = _____

_____ ÷ _____ = _____

_____ ÷ _____ = _____

_____ × _____ = _____

_____ ÷ _____ = _____

_____ ÷ _____ = _____

_____ × _____ = _____

_____ ÷ _____ = _____

_____ ÷ _____ = _____

10.

_____ × _____ = _____

_____ ÷ _____ = _____

_____ ÷ _____ = _____

_____ × _____ = _____

_____ ÷ _____ = _____

_____ ÷ _____ = _____

_____ × _____ = _____

_____ ÷ _____ = _____

_____ ÷ _____ = _____

Extra Practice 3A

Name: _____ Date: _____

Solve. Show your work.

11. Lee puts 54 stickers equally in 6 albums.
How many stickers are there in each album?

12. Mrs. Thomas buys 42 flowers.
She puts the flowers equally into 7 vases.
How many flowers does each vase have?

13. Mr. Li fills 8 pails with a total of 72 liters of water.
    Every pail has the same amount of water.
    How much water does each pail contain?

14. A book has 81 pages in all.
    There are 9 chapters in the book.
    Each chapter contains the same number of pages.
    How many pages does each chapter contain?

15. Jon shares a box of biscuits with 6 other friends.
There are 35 biscuits in the box.
How many biscuits does each child get?

Name: _____   Date: _____

Lesson 6.7   Division: Making Equal Groups

Fill in the missing numbers.

1. _____ × 9 = 72

    72 ÷ 9 = _____

2. _____ × 8 = 24

    24 ÷ 8 = _____

Divide.

3. 56 ÷ 7 = _____

4. 42 ÷ 6 = _____

5. 64 ÷ 8 = _____

6. 81 ÷ 9 = _____

Solve. Show your work.

7. Each boat has 7 sailors.
   There are 63 sailors altogether.
   How many boats are there?

Extra Practice 3A   95

8. There are 48 children participating in the math competition. The children are placed in groups. Each group has 6 children. How many groups are there?

9. Marco has 56 markers. He keeps 8 markers in each box. How many boxes of markers does Marco have?

 **Put on Your Thinking Cap!**

1. Nicole thinks of two numbers.
   Both numbers are 2-digit numbers.
   Both digits are different.
   What are Nicole's numbers?

   Use the clues below to help find her numbers.

   a. 1st number

   Clues
   The sum of its two digits is 10.
   The tens digit is greater than the ones digit.
   You say the number when you count by eights.
   The number is greater than half of 100 but less than 9 × 9.

   Nicole's first number is _____.

   b. 2nd number

   Clues
   The sum of its two digits is 6.
   The tens digit is greater than the ones digit.
   You say the number when you count by sixes.
   You also say it when you count by sevens.
   The number is less than half of 100.

   Nicole's second number is _____.

Extra Practice 3A   97

2. A square table can seat 4 children.

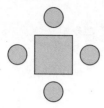

When Mrs. Smith places 2 square tables together, 6 children can sit around the two tables.

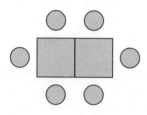

a. If Mrs. Smith places 3 square tables together, how many children can sit around the tables?

b. If she places 4 square tables together, how many children can sit around the tables?

c. If she places 10 square tables together, how many children can sit around the tables? How did you find the answer?

Name: _____   Date: _____

 # Multiplication

Lesson 7.1 Mental Multiplication

Multiply mentally.

1. 4 × 3 = _____
2. 5 × 7 = _____
3. 9 × 2 = _____
4. 8 × 3 = _____
5. 7 × 6 = _____
6. 4 × 9 = _____
7. 10 × 3 = _____
8. 8 × 5 = _____
9. 6 × 9 = _____
10. 7 × 7 = _____
11. 8 × 8 = _____
12. 9 × 9 = _____

Multiply mentally. Fill in the missing numbers.

13. 4 × 60 = 4 × 6 tens
    = _____ tens
    = _____

14. 4 × 600 = 4 × 6 hundreds
    = _____ hundreds
    = _____

15. 7 × 80 = 7 × 8 tens
    = _____ tens
    = _____

16. 7 × 800 = 7 × 8 hundreds
    = _____ hundreds
    = _____

Extra Practice 3A

Name: _____   Date: _____

17. 9 × 50 = 9 × 5 tens

= _____ tens

= _____

18. 9 × 500 = 9 × 5 hundreds

= _____ hundreds

= _____

Multiply mentally.

19. 3 × 40 = _____

20. 3 × 400 = _____

21. 4 × 50 = _____

22. 4 × 500 = _____

23. 4 × 80 = _____

24. 4 × 800 = _____

25. 5 × 90 = _____

26. 5 × 900 = _____

27. 6 × 60 = _____

28. 6 × 600 = _____

29. 8 × 80 = _____

30. 8 × 800 = _____

31. 7 × 30 = _____

32. 7 × 300 = _____

33. 7 × 90 = _____

34. 7 × 900 = _____

35. 8 × 20 = _____

36. 8 × 200 = _____

37. 9 × 40 = _____

38. 9 × 400 = _____

39. 9 × 90 = _____

40. 9 × 900 = _____

Name: _____   Date: _____

Lesson 7.2 Multiplying Without Regrouping

Fill in the missing numbers.

1. 22 × 4 = ?

    _____ ones × 4 = _____ ones

    _____ tens × 4 = _____ tens

    $$\begin{array}{r} 2\,2 \\ \times 4 \\ \hline \square \end{array}$$

2. 31 × 3 = ?

    _____ one × 3 = _____ ones

    _____ tens × 3 = _____ tens

    $$\begin{array}{r} 3\,1 \\ \times 3 \\ \hline \square \end{array}$$

3. 43 × 2 = ?

    _____ ones × 2 = _____ ones

    _____ tens × 2 = _____ tens

    $$\begin{array}{r} 4\,3 \\ \times 2 \\ \hline \square \end{array}$$

4. 11 × 6 = ?

    _____ one × 6 = _____ ones

    _____ ten × 6 = _____ tens

    $$\begin{array}{r} 1\,1 \\ \times 6 \\ \hline \square \end{array}$$

5. 321 × 3 = ?

    _____ one × 3 = _____ ones

    _____ tens × 3 = _____ tens

    _____ hundreds × 3 = _____ hundreds

    $$\begin{array}{r} 3\,2\,1 \\ \times 3 \\ \hline \square \end{array}$$

Extra Practice 3A

Name: _____ Date: _____

6. 324 × 2 = ?

_____ ones × 2 = _____ ones

_____ tens × 2 = _____ tens

_____ hundreds × 2 = _____ hundreds

$$\begin{array}{r} 3\ 2\ 4 \\ \times 2 \\ \hline \end{array}$$

Multiply.

7. $\begin{array}{r} 2\ 4\ 3 \\ \times 2 \\ \hline \end{array}$

8. $\begin{array}{r} 1\ 2\ 2 \\ \times 4 \\ \hline \end{array}$

9. $\begin{array}{r} 2\ 0\ 2 \\ \times 4 \\ \hline \end{array}$

10. $\begin{array}{r} 1\ 1\ 0 \\ \times 5 \\ \hline \end{array}$

11. $\begin{array}{r} 1\ 0\ 0 \\ \times 7 \\ \hline \end{array}$

12. $\begin{array}{r} 1\ 0\ 1 \\ \times 9 \\ \hline \end{array}$

Name: _____ Date: _____

Solve. Show your work.

13. On a visit to a museum, 44 children received souvenirs. Each child received 2 souvenirs. How many souvenirs were given away?

14. Mrs. Raja makes 21 identical hair bands for her dancers. She uses 4 flowers each for each hair band. How many flowers does Mrs. Raja use altogether?

15. Allen prepares 32 desserts. He prepares three times as many sandwiches as desserts. How many sandwiches does Allen prepare?

16. A desk costs $204.
Mrs. Tay buys two desks.
How much does Mrs. Tay pay for the desks?

Name: _____ Date: _____

Lesson 7.3   Multiplying Ones, Tens, and Hundreds with Regrouping (Part 1)

Fill in the missing numbers.

1.   176 × 4 = ?

   Step 1   Multiply the ones by 4.

   _____ ones × 4 = _____ ones

   Regroup the ones.

   _____ ones = _____ tens _____ ones

   Step 2   Multiply the tens by 4.

   _____ tens × 4 = _____ tens

   Add the tens.

   _____ tens + _____ tens = _____ tens

   Regroup the tens.

   _____ tens = _____ hundreds _____ tens

   Step 3   Multiply the hundreds by 4.

   _____ hundred × 4 = _____ hundreds

   Add the hundreds.

   _____ hundreds + _____ hundreds

   = _____ hundreds

   So, 176 × 4 = _____.

Name: _____ **Date:** _____

2.   245 × 3 = ?

　　　Step 1　Multiply the ones by 3.

　　　　　_____ ones × 3 = _____ ones

　　　　　Regroup the ones.

　　　　　_____ ones = _____ ten _____ ones

　　　Step 2　Multiply the tens by 3.

　　　　　_____ tens × 3 = _____ tens

　　　　　Add the tens.

　　　　　_____ tens + _____ ten = _____ tens

　　　　　Regroup the tens.

　　　　　_____ tens = _____ hundred _____ tens

　　　Step 3　Multiply the hundreds by 3.

　　　　　_____ hundreds × 3 = _____ hundreds

　　　　　Add the hundreds.

　　　　　_____ hundreds + _____ hundred

　　　　　= _____ hundreds

　　　　　So, 245 × 3 = _____.

Name: _____ Date: _____

3. 147 × 4 = ?

Step 1 Multiply the ones by 4.

_____ ones × 4 = _____ ones

Regroup the ones.

_____ ones = _____ tens _____ ones

Step 2 Multiply the tens by 4.

_____ tens × 4 = _____ tens

Add the tens.

_____ tens + _____ tens = _____ tens

Regroup the tens.

_____ tens = _____ hundred _____ tens

Step 3 Multiply the hundreds by 4.

_____ hundreds × 4 = _____ hundreds

Add the hundreds.

_____ hundreds + _____ hundred

= _____ hundreds

So, 147 × 4 = _____.

Extra Practice 3A

Name: _____   Date: _____

Multiply.

4.
```
    3 5 8
  ×     2
  ───────
  ┌─────┐
  └─────┘
```

5.
```
    1 6 7
  ×     5
  ───────
  ┌─────┐
  └─────┘
```

6.
```
    1 3 4
  ×     7
  ───────
  ┌─────┐
  └─────┘
```

7.
```
    1 5 2
  ×     6
  ───────
  ┌─────┐
  └─────┘
```

8.
```
    4 9 9
  ×     2
  ───────
  ┌─────┐
  └─────┘
```

9.
```
    2 3 5
  ×     4
  ───────
  ┌─────┐
  └─────┘
```

10.
```
    2 6 9
  ×     2
  ───────
  ┌─────┐
  └─────┘
```

11.
```
    3 5 8
  ×     2
  ───────
  ┌─────┐
  └─────┘
```

Name: _____ Date: _____

12.
    2 4 6
×   4
_____

13.
    1 2 7
×   5
_____

14.
    1 2 6
×   7
_____

15.
    1 8 5
×   5
_____

Solve. Show your work

16. Gigi saves $285 each year.
How much money will she save in 3 years?

Extra Practice 3A 109

Name: _____ Date: _____

17. Jessie imports 458 roses each month. How many roses does she import in 2 months?

18. Rafi bakes 164 snacks a day. How many snacks does he bake in 6 days?

Name: _____ Date: _____

 **Put on Your Thinking Cap!**

Solve. Regroup the ones and tens when you multiply.

How many different solutions can you find for each of the problems below?

Example

a.
```
    2 0
  ×   7
  ─────
  1 4 0
```

b.
```
    7 0
  ×   2
  ─────
  1 4 0
```

c.
```
    3 5
  ×   4
  ─────
  1 4 0
```

1. a.
```
    ☐ ☐
  ×   ☐
  ─────
  1 1 2
```

b.
```
    ☐ ☐
  ×   ☐
  ─────
  1 1 2
```

c.
```
    ☐ ☐
  ×   ☐
  ─────
  1 1 2
```

2. a.
```
    ☐ ☐
  ×   ☐
  ─────
  1 3 6
```

b.
```
    ☐ ☐
  ×   ☐
  ─────
  1 3 6
```

c.
```
    ☐ ☐
  ×   ☐
  ─────
  1 3 6
```

Extra Practice 3A   **111**

Name: _____ Date: _____

Arrange the numbers

3. How many different 3-digit numbers can you make using the numbers below

   8 6 5

   a. if you can use each digit once only?

   b. if you can use each digit more than once?

4. Find the greatest product and the smallest product by using the following four digits. Use each digit only once.

   8 5 4 6

   a. The greatest product   b. The smallest product

112 Chapter 7 Put on Your Thinking Cap!

Name: _____ Date: _____

 # Division

Lesson 8.1 Mental Division

**Think of the multiplication facts for 6, 7, 8, and 9.
Then fill in the missing numbers.**

1. _____ × 6 = 48   48 ÷ 6 = _____

2. _____ × 8 = 72   72 ÷ 8 = _____

3. _____ × 7 = 56   56 ÷ 7 = _____

4. _____ × 9 = 54   54 ÷ 9 = _____

5. _____ × 7 = 49   49 ÷ 7 = _____

6. _____ × 6 = 54   54 ÷ 6 = _____

7. _____ × 8 = 64   64 ÷ 8 = _____

8. _____ × 7 = 63   63 ÷ 7 = _____

9. _____ × 6 = 42   42 ÷ 6 = _____

10. _____ × 9 = 81   81 ÷ 9 = _____

Name: _____ Date: _____

Fill in the blanks.

11.   360 ÷ 9 = _____ tens ÷ 9

    = _____ tens

    = _____

12.   800 ÷ 4 = _____ hundreds ÷ 4

    = _____ hundreds

    = _____

Divide. Use related multiplication facts and patterns to help you.

13.   48 ÷ 8 = _____

14.   480 ÷ 8 = _____

15.   21 ÷ 7 = _____

16.   210 ÷ 7 = _____

17.   36 ÷ 9 = _____

18.   360 ÷ 9 = _____

19.   240 ÷ 6 = _____

20.   420 ÷ 7 = _____

21.   350 ÷ 5 = _____

22.   720 ÷ 9 = _____

23.   810 ÷ 9 = _____

24.   640 ÷ 8 = _____

Name: _____   Date: _____

Lesson 8.2   Quotient and Remainder

**Circle equal groups and find the remainder.
Then fill in the missing numbers.**

1.

4 children share 23 stickers equally.

23 ones ÷ 4 = ☐ R ☐

Quotient = ☐ ones

Remainder = ☐ ones

Each child has _____ stickers.

There are _____ stickers left over.

2. △△△△△△
△△△△△△
△△△△△△
△△△△△△
△△

6 friends share 26 slices of pizza equally.

26 ones ÷ 6 = ☐ R ☐

Quotient = ☐ ones

Remainder = ☐ ones

Each friend has _____ pizza slices.

There are _____ pizza slices left over.

Extra Practice 3A   **115**

Name: _____   Date: _____

Find the missing numbers.

3. 39 ÷ 8 = ☐ R ☐

4. 35 ÷ 4 = ☐ R ☐

5. 59 ÷ 9 = ☐ R ☐

6. 60 ÷ 7 = ☐ R ☐

7. 68 ÷ 8 = ☐ R ☐

8. 70 ÷ 9 = ☐ R ☐

9. 63 ÷ 6 = ☐ R ☐

10. 42 ÷ 5 = ☐ R ☐

11. 28 ÷ 3 = ☐ R ☐

12. 53 ÷ 7 = ☐ R ☐

Name: _____ Date: _____

Lesson 8.3 Odd and Even Numbers

Fill in the missing numbers. Use each digit only once in each number.

1. Kerri uses the digits 7, 5, 4, and 8.
   Help Kerri write down all possible

   a. 4-digit odd numbers

   b. 4-digit even numbers

Odd Numbers	Even Numbers

2. Megan uses the digits 6, 3, 0, and 7.
   Help Megan form the:

   a. greatest 4-digit odd number.

   b. greatest 4-digit even number.

   c. smallest 4-digit odd number.

   d. smallest 4-digit even number.

Extra Practice 3A

3. Talia uses the digits 5, 9, 0, 4, and 8.
   Help Talia form the:

   a. greatest 2-digit odd number.

   b. smallest 2-digit even number.

   c. greatest 3-digit odd number.

   d. greatest 3-digit even number.

   e. smallest 3-digit odd number.

   f. smallest 3-digit even number.

   g. greatest 4-digit even number.

   h. smallest 4-digit odd number.

Lesson 8.4 Division Without Remainder and Regrouping

Divide. Then solve.

1.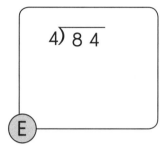
   E

2.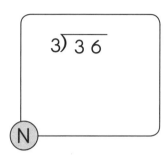
   N

3.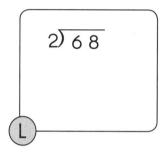
   L

4.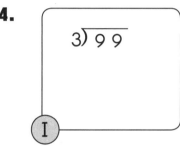
   I

5.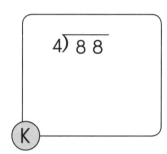
   K

6.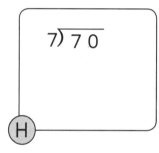
   H

7.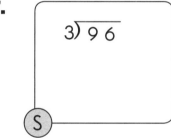
   S

8.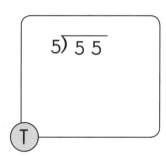
   T

9.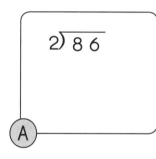
   A

10.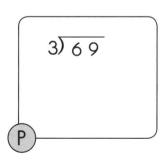
    P

11.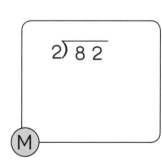
    M

12.
    J

Which animal can carry its home on its back?

___ ___ ___   ___ ___ ___ ___ ___
(11) (10) (21)   (32) (12) (43) (33) (34)

Name: _____   Date: _____

Solve. Show your work.

13. Renee bakes 63 snacks.
She puts them equally into 3 jars.
How many snacks are there in each jar?

14. Calvin arranges 80 chairs into 8 equal rows.
How many chairs are there in each row?

Name: _____ Date: _____

Lesson 8.5 Division with Regrouping in Tens and Ones

Divide. Use base-ten blocks to help you.

1. 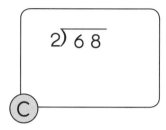 2)68 C

2. 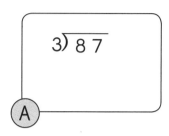 3)87 A

3. 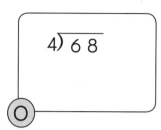 4)68 O

4. 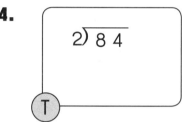 2)84 T

5. 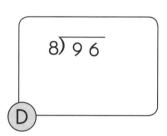 8)96 D

6. 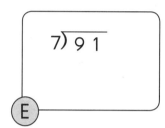 7)91 E

7. 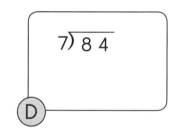 7)84 D

8. 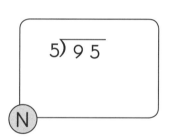 5)95 N

9. 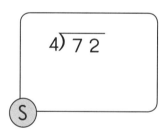 4)72 S

10. 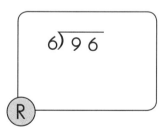 6)96 R

11. 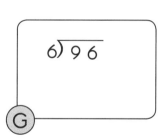 6)96 G

12. 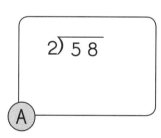 2)58 A

Give one reason why some people do not put an ad in the newspaper when they lose their dog.

Match the letters to the quotients below to find out.

___ ___ ___ ___   ___ ___ ___ , ___
(12) (17) (24) (18)   (34) (29) (19) (14)

___ ___ ___ ___ !
(16) (13) (29) (12)

Solve. Show your work.

13. A grocer sells 72 plums in 3 days.
He sells the same number of plums everyday.
How many plums does the grocer sell in a day?

14. Mr. Tee arranges 64 chairs equally into 4 circles.
How many chairs are there in each circle?

Name: _____ Date: _____

 **Put on Your Thinking Cap!**

1. Sharon is thinking of a number.
It is an even number between 300 and 400.
It is divisible by 5 and also by 9.
What number is Sharon thinking of?

301, 302, 303, ..., 395, 396, 397, 398, 399

Name: _____ Date: _____

2. Granny has some stickers.
If she gives 6 stickers to each of her grandchildren, she will have 5 stickers left.
If she gives 7 stickers to each of her grandchildren, she will need 2 more stickers.

a. How many stickers does Granny have?

b. How many grandchildren does Granny have?

Find the missing numbers.

3.
I am a 2-digit odd number.
I am between 50 and 100.
The difference between my digits is 3.
I do not leave a remainder when divided by 7.

I am _____.

4.
I am a 2-digit odd number.
I am less than 50.
The sum of my digits is 9.
I do not leave a remainder when divided by 5.

I am _____.

Name: _____   Date: _____

 **Using Bar Models: Multiplication and Division**

Lesson 9.1   Real-World Problems: Multiplication

Solve. Draw bar models to help you.

1. A plane has 450 seats.
    There are 4 times as many seats on the train as on the plane.
    How many seats are there on the train?

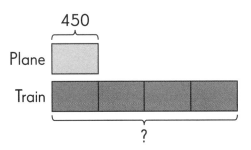

2. A refrigerator costs 5 times as much as a television.
    The television costs $429. What is the cost of the refrigerator?

Extra Practice 3A   **125**

3. Town X is 329 kilometers away from Town Y.
Town Z is 9 times as far from Town Y as Town X is.
How far is Town Z from Town Y?

4. There are 965 marbles in the box.
There are 8 times as many marbles in the container as in the box.
How many marbles are there in the container?

Name: _____ Date: _____

Lesson 9.2 Real-World Problems: Two-Step Problems with Multiplication

Solve. Draw bar models to help you.

1. Lilian sold 457 tickets to the fair.
   Rohani sold 3 times as many tickets as Lilian.

   a. How many tickets did Rohani sell?

   b. How many fewer tickets did Lilian sell than Rohani?

2. The students in Class 3A buy 500 packets of seeds to start an eco-garden. On Monday, they use 27 packets of seeds. On Tuesday, they use twice as many packets of seeds as on Monday. How many packets of seeds do the students have left?

3. Mrs. Johnson buys 68 posts and some wire to make a fence.
Each post costs $7. The wire costs $46.
How much does Mrs. Johnson pay for the posts and the wire?

4. Alice has 168 marbles.
Ben has 4 times as many marbles as Alice. Cindy has 28 more marbles than Ben.

   a. How many marbles does Ben have?

   b. How many marbles does Cindy have?

Name: _____ Date: _____

Lesson 9.3 Real-World Problems: Division

Solve. Draw bar models to help you.

1. At the beach, 6 children pick up a total of 96 seashells.
   They share the seashells equally.
   How many seashells does each child have?

   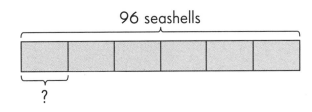

2. Desmond and Melissa collect cards.
   They have 92 cards in all.
   Melissa has three times as many cards as Desmond.
   How many cards does Desmond have?

Extra Practice 3A

Name: _____ Date: _____

3. Lynette spends $95 on a pair of shoes and a purse. The pair of shoes costs 4 times as much as the purse. How much does Lynette pay for the purse?

4. A bookshelf has 84 books on it. There are twice as many non-fiction books as fiction books. How many fiction books are there on the bookshelf?

Name: _____ Date: _____

Lesson 9.4 Real-World Problems: Two-step Problems with Division

Solve. Draw bar models to help you.

1. Sophia prepares 38 cheese sandwiches and 46 tuna sandwiches.
   She puts the sandwiches equally onto 3 platters.
   How many sandwiches are on each platter?

2. Maria has $500. She buys a pair of shoes for $108.
   She gives the rest of the money to her 4 nieces.
   Her nieces share the money equally.

   a. How much money does Maria give to her 4 nieces?

   b. How much does each niece get?

Extra Practice 3A

3. Corrine buys 37 green paper clips and 54 blue paper clips. She puts all the paper clips together and packs them into packets of 7 paper clips each.
How many packets of paper clips are there?

4. Durai buys a dining table and 8 identical chairs for $294. The table costs $198.
How much does each chair cost?

5. A florist buys 4 boxes of carnations.
There are 21 carnations in each box.
The florist puts the carnations into bouquets of 6 carnations each.
How many bouquets of carnations are there?

6. There are 48 boys and 37 girls in a competition.
All the children are grouped into 5 equal teams.
How many children are there on each team?

7. Clifford has 175 angelfish.
   He keeps 126 angelfish and gives the rest to 7 friends.
   Each friend gets the same number of angelfish. How many angelfish does each friend get?

8. Adir buys 6 boxes of apples.
   Each box contains 16 apples.
   He repacks the apples equally into 8 cartons.
   How many apples are there in each carton?

Put on Your Thinking Cap!

1. A store records the sales of its toys in the table below.

Month	Number of Toys Sold
January	180
February	90 more than in January
March	3 times as many as in February
April	320 fewer than in March

a. How many toys are sold in February?

b. How many toys are sold in March?

c. How many toys are sold in April?

d. How many toys are sold altogether during the four months?

Name: _____ Date: _____

2. Teresa and Nancy make 135 pins for a fund-raising project.
Teresa makes 37 more pins than Nancy.
How many pins does Teresa make?

3. Alex and Jim have equal amounts of money.
Each day, Alex spends $5 and Jim spends $3.
When Alex has $8 left, Jim has 4 times as much money left as Alex.
How much money does each boy have at first?

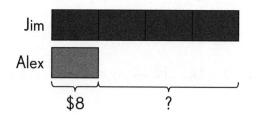

Name: _____ Date: _____

4. Find an easy way to add the numbers from 1 to 10.

$$1 + 2 + 3 + 4 + 5 + 6 + 7 + 8 + 9 + 10$$

Each pair of numbers shown above has a sum of 11.

So, $1 + 2 + 3 + 4 + 5 + 6 + 7 + 8 + 9 + 10 = 11 \times 5$
$= 55$

Using the above method, find the sums of the following numbers.

a. $1 + 2 + 3 + 4 + 5 + ... + 17 + 18 + 19 + 20$

b. $1 + 2 + 3 + 4 + 5 + ... + 37 + 38 + 39 + 40$

c. $11 + 22 + 33 + 44 + 55 + 66 + 77 + 88 + 99$

5. The table explains divisibility tests. You can tell if a number is divisible by 2, 3, 4, 5, 9, or 10 by looking at the number's digits.

A number is divisible by ...	...if...
2	the ones digit is even (0, 2, 4, 6, or 8).
5	the ones digit is 0 or 5.
10	the ones digit is 0.
4	the last two digits of the number is divisible by 4.
3	the sum of the digits of the number is divisible by 3.
9	the sum of the digits of the number is divisible by 9.

Example

The number 9,864 is divisible by 9 because the sum of the digits is divisible by 9.
9 + 8 + 6 + 4 = 27
27 is divisible by 9.

Fill in the missing digits to make the statements <u>true</u>.

a. 7 _____ 6 is divisible by 3.

b. 9 _____ 2 is divisible by 4.

c. 27 _____ is divisible by 5.

d. 9 _____ 4 is divisible by 3.

e. 59 _____ is divisible by 4.

f. 53 _____ is divisible by 2.

g. 6 _____ 4 is divisible by 9.

h. 7 _____ 8 is divisible by 4.

i. _____ 57 is divisible by 9.

j. 9 _____ 8 is divisible by 9.

Name: _____ Date: _____

Mid-Year Test Prep

Multiple Choice (20 × 2 points = 40 points)

Fill in the circle next to the correct answer.

1. Which of the following numbers has the digit 7 in the thousands place?

   Ⓐ 6,970   Ⓑ 7,906   Ⓒ 9,607   Ⓓ 9,760

2. What is the value of the digit 8 in the number 5,893?

   Ⓐ 8 ones   Ⓑ 8 tens
   Ⓒ 8 hundreds   Ⓓ 8 thousands

3. 3,085 is 10 tens more than _____.

   Ⓐ 2,985   Ⓑ 3,075   Ⓒ 3,095   Ⓓ 3,185

4. Nine thousand, four hundred three written in standard form is _____.

   Ⓐ 9,034   Ⓑ 9,043   Ⓒ 9,403   Ⓓ 9,430

5. In 5,786, the digit 5 has the same value as _____.

   Ⓐ 5 × 1   Ⓑ 5 × 10
   Ⓒ 5 × 100   Ⓓ 5 × 1,000

Extra Practice 3A   **139**

Name: _____ Date: _____

6. Which of these numbers is the greatest even number?

　Ⓐ　6,000 + 800 + 20 + 4

　Ⓑ　6,000 + 700 + 80 + 8

　Ⓒ　6,000 + 800 + 50 + 8

　Ⓓ　6,000 + 700 + 60 + 6

7. Complete the number pattern:

　189, 209, 249, 329, _____, 809

　Ⓐ 429　　Ⓑ 449　　Ⓒ 489　　Ⓓ 569

8. When 328 is added to 79 × 4, the value is _____.

　Ⓐ 316　　Ⓑ 407　　Ⓒ 411　　Ⓓ 644

9. I divide a number by 3 and subtract 85 from the quotient to make 190. What is the number?

　Ⓐ 35　　Ⓑ 92　　Ⓒ 315　　Ⓓ 825

10. Divide 87 by 6. The remainder is _____.

　Ⓐ 2　　Ⓑ 3　　Ⓒ 4　　Ⓓ 5

11. 36 × 2 = ☐ × 4. The missing number is _____.

　Ⓐ 12　　Ⓑ 14　　Ⓒ 16　　Ⓓ 18

Name: _____ Date: _____

12. 30 tens is _____ more than 49 fives.

  (A) 19   (B) 55   (C) 75   (D) 251

13. What is the product of 346 and 9?

  (A) 300 + 14

  (B) 3,000 + 14

  (C) 300 + 100 + 4

  (D) 3,000 + 100 + 14

14. Jane has $298.
Linda has $47 more than Jane.
How much money do they have in all?

  (A) $251   (B) $345   (C) $549   (D) $643

15. Maria puts 6 tarts in each box.
Maria has 56 boxes of tarts with 4 tarts left over.
How many tarts does she have?

  (A) 310   (B) 332   (C) 336   (D) 340

16. Ian buys some magazines for $8 each.
He gives the cashier $100 and receives $4 change.
How many magazines does Ian buy?

  (A) 8   (B) 9   (C) 11   (D) 12

Extra Practice 3A

Name: _____   Date: _____

17. Nara has a total of 96 blue and red beads. She has three times as many blue beads as red beads. How many red beads does Nara have?

Ⓐ 24   Ⓑ 32   Ⓒ 93   Ⓓ 288

18. There are 120 pages in a book. Joni reads 12 pages each day. How many pages are left to read after 6 days?

Ⓐ 20   Ⓑ 48   Ⓒ 72   Ⓓ 108

19. There are a total of 15 bicycles and tricycles. There are 36 wheels in all. How many tricycles are there?

Ⓐ 6   Ⓑ 7   Ⓒ 8   Ⓓ 9

20. $2 \times \boxplus + 2 \times \pentagon + \triangle = 67$

$\boxplus + \pentagon = 30$

$\pentagon + \triangle = 25$

$\boxplus = $ _____

Ⓐ 16   Ⓑ 14   Ⓒ 12   Ⓓ 8

Name: _____ Date: _____

Short Answer (20 × 2 points = 40 points)

Write your answer in the space given.

21. Write the number five thousand, six hundred nine in standard form.

Answer: _____

22. The value of the digit 7 in 3,786 is _____.

Answer: _____

23. Multiply 124 by 8.

Answer: _____

24. The product of two numbers is 91.
If one of the numbers is 7, the other number is _____.

Answer: _____

Extra Practice 3A

Name: _____ Date: _____

25. Use each digit below only once to form the greatest 4-digit even number.

[4] [7] [6] [3]

Answer: _____

26. Find the greatest product of a 3-digit number and a 1-digit number using each digit below only once.

[3] [5] [6] [7]

☐ ☐ ☐
×   ☐
―――――

Answer: _____

27. 7 groups of 150 is _____ less than 9 groups of 130.

Answer: _____

144   Mid-Year Test Prep

Name: _____ Date: _____

28. A refrigerator costs $295 more than an oven costs.
The oven costs $325.
How much does the refrigerator cost?

Answer: $ _____

29. When a number is divided by 5, it has a quotient of 136 and a remainder of 3. What is the number?

Answer: _____

30. Sophia packs 84 crackers equally into 6 boxes.
How many crackers are in each box?

Answer: _____ crackers

Name: _____ **Date:** _____

31. Muthu has 4 times as much money as Raja has.
Muthu has $92. How much money does Raja have?

Answer: $_____

32. Joel has 169 marbles.

Leon has 3 times as many marbles as Joel.

They have _____ marbles in all.

Answer: _____

33. Complete the following number pattern.

1, 2, 3, 5, 8, 13, 21, _____, _____

Answer: _____

Name: _____ Date: _____

34. Find the sum of $1 + 2 + 3 + 4 + 5 + \cdots + 97 + 98 + 99 + 100$.

Answer: _____

35. What is the missing number?

Answer: _____

36. Mr. Warren pays a total of $240 for a table and 5 chairs.

Each chair costs $9. The table costs $_____.

Answer: $_____

Extra Practice 3A   147

37. The sum of two numbers is 300.
One number is 206 more than the other number.
What is the value of the smaller number?

Answer: _____

38. Pauline has 104 stamps.

Joyce has 36 stamps fewer than Pauline.

Fiona has 58 stamps more than Joyce.

Fiona has _____ stamps.

Answer: _____

Name: _____ **Date:** _____

39. ☐☐☐☐ + △ = 172

◻◻ + △ = 100

△ = _____

Answer: _____

40. Grace has 78 stickers.
She has 3 times as many stickers as Matthew.
How many stickers do they have altogether?

Answer: _____ stickers

Extra Practice 3A **149**

Name: _____   Date: _____

Extended Response (5 × 4 points = 20 points)

Solve. Show your work.

41. A cafeteria sells 148 muffins.
They sell 65 more sandwiches than muffins.
How many sandwiches and muffins does the cafeteria sell?

Answer: _____ muffins and sandwiches

42. Roger bakes 165 muffins.
After selling 87 muffins, he gives the remainder equally to 6 neighbors.
How many muffins does each neighbor receive?

Answer: _____ muffins

Name: _____ **Date:** _____

43. Anne has 37 books.
Bobby has 4 times as many books as Anne.
Clara has 69 fewer books than Bobby.
How many books does Clara have?

Answer: _____ books

44. On Sunday, a florist sells 96 roses.
She sells 4 times as many roses as lilies.
She sells 78 more carnations than lilies.
How many carnations does the florist sell?

Answer: _____ carnations

Extra Practice 3A

45. There are 765 marbles in a box.
There are twice as many blue marbles as green marbles.
There are 3 times as many red marbles as blue marbles.
How many red marbles are there in the box?

Answer: _____ red marbles

Answers

Chapter 1

Lesson 1.1
1. 5,005
2. 3,029
3. 7,400
4. 9,919
5. 8,088
6. six thousand nine hundred
7. three thousand seventy-seven
8. four thousand, six hundred twenty-one
9. two thousand, one hundred ninety-eight
10. <u>6</u> thousands <u>0</u> hundreds <u>9</u> tens <u>6</u> ones = <u>6,096</u>
11. <u>9</u> thousands <u>3</u> hundreds <u>4</u> tens <u>0</u> ones = <u>9,340</u>
12. 3,965; 4,065; 4,165
13. 7,823; 7,923; 8,023
14. 3,798; 4,798; 5,798
15. 6,321; 7,321; 8,321
16. 3,874; 3,864; 3,854
17. 5,743; 5,732; 5,722
18. 6,205; 5,205; 4,205
19. 4,127; 3,127; 2,127
20. 8,915
21. 9,427
22. 8,365
23. 6,728
24. 5,761
25. 7,495

Lesson 1.2

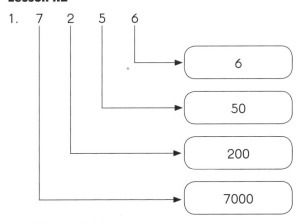

2. 300; 9; 8,000; 40
3. tens; 90
4. 6; hundreds
5. 2; thousands
6. ones; 8
7. 900
8. 2,000
9. 8
10. 3,192
11. 1,889

Lesson 1.3
1. 2,713
2. 4,566
3. 6,256
4. 4,100
5. 8,300
6. 8,875
7. 8,928
8. 7,040
9. 7,533
10. 10
11. 400
12. 3,000
13. 20
14. 100
15. 1,000
16. 500
17. 2,000
18. 700
19. 1,000
20. 100
21. 2,000
22. 2,476
23. 8,800
24. >
25. >
26. <
27. <
28. 5,237, 3,725, 3,572, 3,275
29. 8,496, 8,694, 8,946, 8,964
30. 4,065, 4,265
31. 7,799, 7,779
32. 4,580, 8,580
33. 6,225, 6,175
34. The <u>pumpkin</u> is heavier than the <u>watermelon</u>.
35. Container <u>X</u> has more water than Container <u>Y</u>.
36. Building <u>A</u> is taller than Building <u>B</u>.
37. Television set <u>P</u> costs more than television set <u>Q</u>.

Put on Your Thinking Cap!

Thinking skill: Comparing, Identify patterns and relationships
Strategy: Guess and check

1. Clue 1: 4-digit number

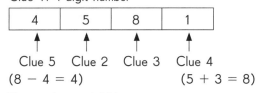

Clue 5   Clue 2   Clue 3   Clue 4
(8 − 4 = 4)   (5 + 3 = 8)

The number is 4,581.

2. 36, 49, 64
3. 1,600, 2,200, 2,900

Thinking skill: Comparing, Identify patterns and relationships
Strategy: Guess and check

4. 18
5. 4,067
6. 7,640
7. 96

Extra Practice 3A 153

Chapter 2

Lesson 2.1

1. 36 + 50 = 86
   86 + 7 = 93
   So, 36 + 57 = 93
   (57 → 50, 7)

2. 19 + 50 = 69
   69 + 6 = 75
   So, 19 + 56 = 75
   (56 → 50, 6)

3. 15 + 50 = 65
   65 − 2 = 63
   So, 15 + 48 = 63
   (50 → 48, 2)

4. 26 + 50 = 76
   76 − 3 = 73
   So, 26 + 47 = 73
   (50 → 47, 3)

5. 84
6. 83
7. 84
8. 105
9. 114
10. 103

Lesson 2.2

1. 73 − 50 = 23
   23 − 8 = 15
   73 − 58 = 15
   (58 → 50, 8)

2. 84 − 30 = 54
   54 − 7 = 47
   84 − 37 = 47
   (37 → 30, 7)

3. 94 − 50 = 44
   44 − 5 = 39
   94 − 55 = 39
   (55 → 50, 5)

4. 75 − 40 = 35
   35 + 2 = 37
   So, 75 − 38 = 37
   (40 → 38, 2)

5. 83 − 50 = 33
   33 + 5 = 38
   So, 83 − 45 = 38
   (50 → 45, 5)

6. 62
7. 25
8. 47
9. 27
10. 32
11. 47

Lesson 2.3

1. 38 + 100 = 138
   138 − 5 = 133
   So, 38 + 95 = 133
   (100 → 95, 5)

2. 47 + 100 = 147
   147 − 3 = 144
   So, 47 + 98 = 145
   (100 → 98, 2)

3. 86 + 100 = 186
   186 − 4 = 182
   So, 86 + 96 = 182
   (100 → 96, 4)

4. 78 + 100 = 178
   178 − 1 = 177
   So, 78 + 99 = 177
   (100 → 99, 1)

5. 66 + 100 = 166
   166 − 2 = 164
   So, 66 + 98 = 164
   (100 → 98, 2)

6. 124
7. 113
8. 145
9. 168
10. 170
11. 183
12. 151
13. 131
14. 141
15. 176

Lesson 2.4

1. 140; 100
2. 660; 700
3. 1,100; 1,000
4. 8,570; 8,600
5. 4,400; 4,400
6. 800
7. 500
8. 600
9. 8,000
10. 849; 750
11. 7,649; 7,550
12. 1,000; 300; 500; Yes
13. 780 + 230 = 1,010
    780 is about 800
    230 is about 200
    800 + 200 = 1,000
    So, 780 + 230 is about 1,000
    1,010 is close to 1,000, so the answer is reasonable.
14. 748 − 319 = 429
    748 is about 700
    319 is about 300
    700 − 300 = 400
    So, 748 − 319 is about 400
    400 is close to 429, so the answer is reasonable.
15. 527 − 288 = 239
    527 is about 500
    288 is about 300
    500 − 300 = 200
    So, 527 − 288 is about 200
    200 is close to 239, so the answer is reasonable.

Lesson 2.5

1. $268 + 323 = \underline{591}$
    $\underline{200} + \underline{300} = \underline{500}$
    The estimated sum is $\underline{500}$.
    The answer $\underline{591}$ is reasonable.

2. $479 + 624 = \underline{1{,}103}$
    $\underline{400} + \underline{600} = \underline{1{,}000}$
    The estimated sum is $\underline{1{,}000}$.
    The answer $\underline{1{,}103}$ is reasonable.

3. $574 - 296 = \underline{278}$
    $\underline{500} - \underline{200} = \underline{300}$
    The estimated difference is $\underline{300}$.
    Yes. The answer 278 is reasonable.

4. $916 - 378 = \underline{538}$
    $\underline{900} - \underline{300} = \underline{600}$
    The estimated difference is $\underline{600}$.
    Yes. The answer 538 is reasonable.

5. $260 + 350 = \underline{610}$
    $\underline{200} + \underline{300} = \underline{500}$
    The estimated sum is $\underline{500}$.
    Yes. The answer 610 is reasonable.

6. $425 + 272 = \underline{697}$
    $\underline{400} + \underline{200} = \underline{600}$
    The estimated sum is $\underline{600}$.
    Yes. The answer 697 is reasonable.

7. $590 - 466 = \underline{124}$
    $\underline{500} - \underline{400} = \underline{100}$
    The estimated difference is $\underline{100}$.
    Yes. The answer 124 is reasonable.

8. $780 - 690 = \underline{90}$
    $\underline{700} - \underline{600} = \underline{100}$
    The estimated difference is $\underline{100}$.
    Yes. The answer 90 is reasonable.

9. Answers vary.
    Sample:
    136 is about 100.
    $100 \times 2 = 200$
    $200 + 100 = 300$
    Beatrice and her brother have about 300 books altogether.

10. Answers vary.
    Sample:
    548 is about 500.
    470 is about 400.
    $500 + 400 = 900$
    The grocer sells abouit 900 fruit altogether.

11. Answers vary.
    Sample:
    650 is about 600.
    480 is about 400.
    $600 - 400 = 200$
    The difference is about 200 meters.

Put on Your Thinking Cap!

1. Thinking skill: Identifying patterns and relationships
    $134 + 53 = \underline{187}$
    $\underline{78} + 47 = \underline{125}$
    $22 + \underline{54} = \underline{76}$
    $\underline{125} - 49 = \underline{76}$

2. 492
3. 309
4. 346
5. 682
6. 334
7. 204

    Thinking skill: Identifying patterns and relationships
    Strategy: Look for a pattern

8. 11; 16; 22
9. 26; 37; 50
10. 32; 64; 128

Chapter 3

Lesson 3.1

1. 4,999
2. 2,779
3. 7,896
4. 8,798
5. 3,746
6. 4,678
7. 5,558
8. 5,869
9. 7,989
10. 4,678
11. 8086
12. 7,937
13. 5,404
14. 8,139
15. 9,824
16. 6,836

Lesson 3.2

1. 12 hundreds = 1 thousand 2 hundreds
2. 14 hundreds = 1 thousand 3 hundreds
3. 16 hundreds = 1 thousand 6 hundreds
4. 18 hundreds = 1 thousand 8 hundreds
5. 13 hundreds = 1 thousand 3 hundreds
6. 3,459
7. 4,119
8. 7,465
9. 9,219

10. 8,559   11. 9,789
12. 6,384   13. 9,459
14. 9,298   15. 9,789

Lesson 3.3

1. 1,433   2. 1,234
3. 1,525   4. 1,515
5. 6,634   6. 7,320
7. 9,065   8. 8,218
9. 9,173   10. 9,224
11. 6,413   12. 6,212
13. 8,455   14. 8,312
15. 9,232   16. 6,642
17. 8,211   18. 5,110
19. $1,346 + $452 = $1,798
    Durai paid $1,798 in all.
20. 1,253 + 1,624 = 2,877
    There are 2,877 students.
21. 1,034 + 242 = 1,276
    Mr. Li has 1,276 sheep.
22. $1,008 + $1,860 = $2,868
    Mr. George spent $2,868 on the plasma TV.
23. 2486 + 3,787 = 6,273
    They collected 6,273 gifts in all.
24. 4,767 + 4,594 = 9,361
    The library has 9,361 books.
25. 4,857 + 256 = 5,113
    There are 5,113 chickens and ducks at the farm.
26. 1,464 + 1,867 = 3,331
    The baker baked 3,331 rolls on Sunday.

Put on Your Thinking Cap!

1. 120; 80   2. 160; 30
3. Thinking skill: Identifying patterns and relationships, Comparing
   Answers vary.
   Sample:
   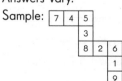

4. a.
$$\begin{array}{r} 1,046 \\ + 2,357 \\ \hline 3,403 \end{array}$$

b.
$$\begin{array}{r} 7,651 \\ + 2,340 \\ \hline 9,991 \end{array}$$

5. Thinking skill: Identifying patterns and relationships
   Strategy: Use guess and check, Make a list
   Use 3 digits to make 19.
   2 + 8 + 9 = 19
   3 + 7 + 9 = 19
   4 + 6 + 9 = 19
   The 3-digit number is greater than 500. The tens digit is the greatest. So, the tens digit is 9.
   Possible numbers: 892   793   694
   The difference between the hundreds digit and the ones digit is 6.
   8 − 2 = 6
   7 − 3 = 4
   6 − 4 = 2
   John's number is 892.

Chapter 4

Lesson 4.1

1. 2,321   2. 6,352
3. 3,444   4. 2,244
5. 5,621   6. 4,031
7. 3,112   8. 3523
9. ⓐ420 378 178 ⓑ650
   650 − 420 = 230
10. ⓐ900 145 ⓑ575 165
    900 − 575 = 325

Lesson 4.2

1. 16   2. 13
3. 18   4. 17
5. 12   6. 1,820
7. 3,713   8. 3,442
9. 810

Lesson 4.3

1. 12
2. 15
3. 13
4. 14
5. 16
6. 19
7. 1,764
8. 4,784
9. 2,689
10. 5,388
11. 4,418
12. 3,758
13. 1,648

Lesson 4.4

1. 680
2. 980
3. 4,759
4. 1,165
5. 520
6. 1,746
7. 2,414
8. 3,064
9. 3,537
10. 5,676
11. 363
12. 3,818
13. 274
    A PORCUPINE
14. 4,005 − 726 = 3,279
    Mrs. Jones needs 3,279 more pencils.
15. $2,050 − $1,598 = $452
    Lena has $452 left.
16. 3,670 − 1,982 = 1,688
    There are 1,688 cows.
17. $3,000 − $1,346 = $1,654
    Mr. Rajan saves $1,654 every month.
18. 5,870 − 2,570 = 3,300
    The difference is 3,300 liters.
19. 3,058 − 1,735 = 1,323
    There were 1,323 fewer children than adults at the performance.
20. 1,260 − 985 = 275
    Mr. Bema needs 275 kilograms of flour.

Put on Your Thinking Cap!

1. 500 − 220 = 280
   280 ÷ 2 = 140
   140 + 220 = 360
   The numbers are 140 and 360.

2. Thinking skill: Comparing, Identifying patterns and relationships

   a.
   ```
     7, 6 5 4
   − 1, 0 2 3
     ─────────
     6, 6 3 1
   ```

   b.
   ```
     2, 0 3 4
   − 1, 7 6 5
     ─────────
     0, 2 6 9
   ```

3. a. Sondhi's score: 225 + 368 + 368 = 961
      Larry's score: 350 + 264 + 264 = 878
      Sondhi scores more points.
      No, he scores less than 1,000 points.
   b. Strategy: Use guess and check
      Moe's score: 368 + 368 + 264 = 1000
      He has hit 2 roosters and 1 rabbit.

4. a. Thinking skill: Comparing
      Strategy: Use guess and check, Make a list
      The first digit must be either 7 or 8.
      List: 7,348, 7,384, 7,438, 7,483, 7,834,
            7,843 8,347, 8,374, 8,437, 8,473,
            8,734, 8,743
      There are twelve 4-digit numbers greater than 7,000.
   b. The greatest four-digit number is 8,743.
      The least four-digit number is 7,348.
      8,743 − 7,348 = 1,395
      The difference is 1,395.

Chapter 5

Lesson 5.1 (Part 1)

1.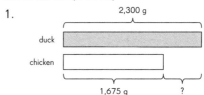

   2,300 − 1,675 = 625
   The duck is 625 grams heavier than the chicken.

2.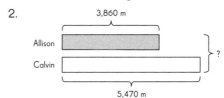

   5,470 + 3,860 = 9,330
   They jog 9,330 meters altogether.

3.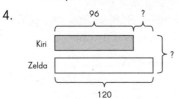

   a. 457 + 686 = 1,143
   They sell 1,143 flags in all.
   b. 686 − 457 = 229
   Tracy. She sells 229 more flags than John.

4.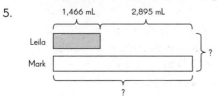

   a. 120 − 96 = 24
   Zelda makes 24 more bookmarks than Kiri.
   b. 96 + 120 = 216
   They make 216 bookmarks altogether.

5.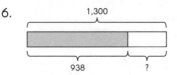

   a. 1,466 + 2,689 = 4,361
   Mark drinks 4,361 milliliters of water.
   b. 1,466 + 4,361 = 5,827
   They drink 5,827 milliliters of water altogether.

6.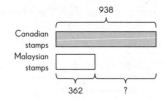

   a. 1,300 − 938 = 362
   Brad has 362 Malaysian stamps.

   b. 938 − 362 = 576
   He has fewer Malaysian stamps.
   He has 576 fewer Malaysian stamps than Canadian stamps.

7.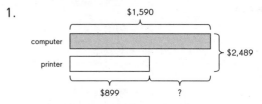

   a. The dining set is less expensive.
   b. $2,500 − $1,999 = $501
   It is $501 less expensive.

Lesson 5.1 (Part 2)

1.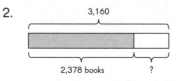

   a. $1,590 − $899 = $691
   The printer is $691 less expensive than the computer.
   b. $1,590 + $899 = $2,489
   The two items cost $2,489 altogether.

2.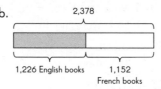

   a. 3,160 − 2,378 = 782
   There are 782 magazines.
   b.

   2,378 − 1,226 = 1,152
   There are 1,152 French books.

3.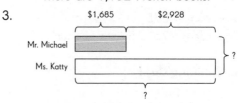

   a. $1,685 + $2,928 = $4,613
   Ms. Katty has $4,613.
   b. $1,685 + $4,613 = $6,298
   They have $6,298 in all.

4.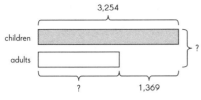

a. 3,254 − 1,369 = 1,885
   There are 1,885 adults at the concert.
b. 3,254 + 1,885 = 5,139
   There are 5,139 people at the concert altogether.

Lesson 5.1 (Part 3)

1.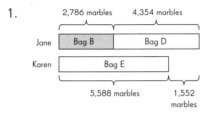

   a. 2,786 + 4,354 = 7,140
      Jane has more marbles.
   b. 7,140 − 5,588 = 1,552
      She has 1,552 more marbles.

2.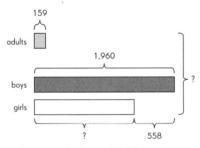

   1,960 − 558 = 1,402
   There are 1,402 girls.
   159 + 1,960 + 1,402 = 3,521
   There are 3,521 people in the school.

3.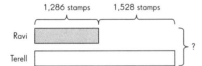

   1,286 + 1,528 = 2,814
   Terell has 2,814 stamps.
   1,286 + 2,814 = 4,100
   They have 4,100 stamps in all.

Put on Your Thinking Cap!

1. Thinking Skill: Analyzing parts and wholes
   Solution: Answers vary.
   Sample:

2. Strategy: Use a model
   Solution:
   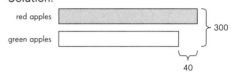

   300 − 40 = 260
   260 ÷ 2 = 130
   Teresa has 130 green apples.

3. Strategy: Use guess and check, Make a list
   The number is greater than 8,000.
   The first digit is either 8 or 9.
   The sum of the thousands digit and the tens digit is 10.
   9 _____ 1 _____ or 8 _____ 2 _____
   The sum of all the digits is 16.
   9 + 1 + 6 + 0 = 16
   9 + 1 + 4 + 2 = 16
   8 + 2 + 6 + 0 = 16
   8 + 2 + 4 + 2 = 16
   The difference between the hundreds digit and the ones digit is 6.
   9,610   9,016   8,620   8,026
   The difference between the thousands digit and the hundreds digit is 3.
   9 − 6 = 3   9 − 0 = 9
   8 − 6 = 2   8 − 0 = 8
   Tashi's number is 9,610.

Test Prep for Chapters 1 to 5

1. D   2. B   3. D
4. A   5. B   6. D
7. C   8. D   9. B
10. D
11. six thousand, nine thundred ninety-nine
12. 200   13. tens
14. 5,625   15. 3,078
16. 3,333   17. 530

Extra Practice 3A 159

18. 333   19. 455
20. 284 or 356 or 428
21.
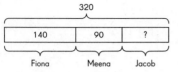
140 + 90 = 230
320 − 230 = 90
Jacob gets 90 seashells.

22.
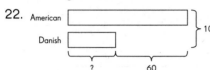
100 − 60 = 40
40 ÷ 2 = 20
Kerrie has 20 Danish stamps.

23.
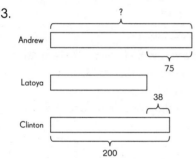
200 − 38 = 162
Latoya has 163 cards.
162 + 75 = 237
Andrew has 237 cards.

24. Answers vary.
Possible answers:
a. Both numbers are 4-digit numbers.
b. In 5,726, the value of digit 7 is 700.
In 5,672, the value of digit 7 is 70.

Chapter 6

Lesson 6.1
1. 9 × 3 = 27
2. 7 × 5 = 35
3. 6 × 4 = 24
4. 8 × 10 = 80
5. 16
6. 16
7. 0
8. 18
9. 28
10. 40
11. 60
12. 21
13. <u>4</u> × 5 = <u>5</u> × 4 = 20
14. <u>8</u> × 3 = 3 × <u>8</u> = 24
15. 10 × <u>9</u> = <u>9</u> × 10 = 90
16. <u>9</u> × 5 = 5 × <u>9</u> = 45
17. <u>8</u> × 2 = 16
18. <u>9</u> × 3 = 27
19. 4 × <u>9</u> = 36
20. 5 × <u>5</u> = 25

Lesson 6.2
1. a. 18; 30   b. 30; 48; 54; 60
2. a. 12   b. 24
   c. 36   d. 48
   e. 3   f. 7
   g. 9, 54   h. 6, 6
3. a. 5
   b. 7 × 6 = <u>42</u>; 7 × 6 = 5 × 6 + <u>2</u> × 6
   c. 2; 4; 12 + 24 = <u>2</u> × 6 + <u>4</u> × 6; 6; 36
   d. 3; 6; 3
4. 4 × 6 = 24
   The four children have 24 pencils in all.
5. 8 × 6 = 48
   He keeps 48 birds in 8 cages.
6. 7 × 6 = 42
   Jason can make 42 bookmarks in 7 hours.
7. 9 × $6 = $54
   Nine dolls cost $54.

Lesson 6.3
1. 6 × 7 = 42   2. 8 × 7 = 56
3. 14   4. 28
5. 35   6. 56
7. 7   8. 9
9. 3, 3   10. 0, 0
11. 4   12. 3
13. 6 × 7 = 42
    There are 42 children in six teams.
14. 36 + 6 = 42
    6 × 7 = 42
    The number is 6.

Lesson 6.4
1. 24; 32; 40
2. 48; 56; 64; 80
3.

×	1	3	5	9	8	7	4	6	10
8	8	24	40	72	64	56	32	48	80

4. 8; 16   5. 7
6. 5; 5   7. 5; 5; 80

8. $7 \times \$8 = \$56$
   Keenan spends $56 in a week.
9. $9 \times 8 = 72$
   Mrs. Li gives 72 storybooks altogether.

Lesson 6.5

1.

×	1	3	5	9	8	7	4	6	10
9	9	27	45	81	72	63	36	54	90

2. $9 \times 9 =$ 5 groups of 9 + <u>4</u> groups of 9
   $= \underline{45} + \underline{36}$
   $= \underline{81}$
   OR
   $9 \times 9 =$ 10 groups of 9 − <u>1</u> group of 9
   $= \underline{90} - \underline{9}$
   $= \underline{81}$

3. $9 \times \$4 = \$36$
   Pam pays $36 in all.

4. $56 + 7 = 63$
   $7 \times 9 = 63$
   The number is 7.

Lesson 6.6

1.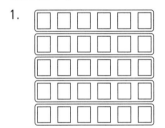
   6; 6

2.
   8; 8

3.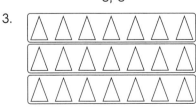
   7; 7

4.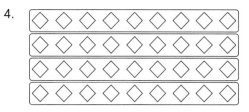
   9; 9

5. 8; 8
6. 9; 9
7. 6; 6
8. 7; 7

9.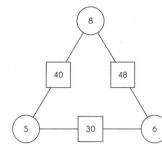
   $5 \times 8 = 40$
   $40 \div 5 = 8$
   $40 \div 8 = 5$
   $6 \times 8 = 48$
   $48 \div 8 = 6$
   $48 \div 6 = 8$
   $5 \times 6 = 30$
   $30 \div 5 = 6$
   $30 \div 6 = 5$

10.
    $7 \times 6 = 42$
    $42 \div 7 = 6$
    $42 \div 6 = 7$
    $9 \times 6 = 54$
    $54 \div 6 = 9$
    $54 \div 9 = 6$
    $7 \times 9 = 63$
    $63 \div 7 = 9$
    $63 \div 9 = 7$

11. $54 \div 6 = 9$
    There are 9 stickers in each album.
12. $42 \div 7 = 6$
    Each vase has 6 flowers.
13. $72 \div 8 = 9$
    Each pail contains 9 liters of water.
14. $81 \div 9 = 9$
    Each chapter contains 9 pages.
15. $6 + 1 = 7$
    $35 \div 7 = 5$
    Each child gets 5 biscuits.

Lesson 6.7

1. 8; 8   2. 3; 3
3. 8   4. 7
5. 8   6. 9
7. $63 \div 7 = 9$
   There are 9 boats.

Extra Practice 3A **161**

8. $48 \div 6 = 8$
   There are 8 groups.
9. $56 \div 8 = 7$
   Marco has 7 boxes of markers.

Put on Your Thinking Cap!

Strategy: Make a list

1. a. $6 + 4 = 10$
      $7 + 3 = 10$
      $8 + 2 = 10$
      $9 + 1 = 10$
      The tens digit is greater than the ones digit.
      Possible numbers: 64, 73, 82, 91
      The number can be divided by 8 exactly.
      It is more than 50 but less than 81.
      Nicole's first number is 64.
   b. $6 + 0 = 6$
      $5 + 1 = 6$
      $4 + 2 = 6$
      The tens digit is greater than the ones digit.
      Possible numbers: 60, 51, 42
      It can be divided by 6 or 7 exactly.
      It is less than 0.
      Nicole's second number is 42.

2. Thinking skill: Identifying patterns and relationships
   Strategy: Look for a pattern
   a.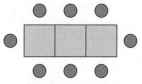
      8 children can sit around the tables.
   b.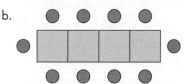
      10 children can sit around the tables.
   c.
No. of tables	No. of children	Pattern
1	4	$1 \times 2 + 2 = 4$
2	6	$2 \times 2 + 2 = 6$
3	8	$3 \times 2 + 2 = 8$
4	10	$4 \times 2 + 2 = 10$
10	22	$10 \times 2 + 2 = 22$

   22 children can sit around 10 tables.
   Find the answer by observing a pattern.

Chapter 7

Lesson 7.1

1. 12   2. 35   3. 18
4. 24   5. 42   6. 36
7. 30   8. 40   9. 54
10. 49 11. 64 12. 81
13. 24; 240   14. 24; 2,400
15. 56; 560   16. 56; 5,600
17. 45; 450   18. 45; 4,500
19. 120   20. 1,200
21. 200   22. 2,000
23. 320   24. 3,200
25. 450   26. 4,500
27. 360   28. 3,600
29. 640   30. 6,400
31. 210   32. 2,100
33. 630   34. 6,300
35. 160   36. 1,600
37. 360   38. 3,600
39. 810   40. 8,100

Lesson 7.2

1. 2 ones × 4 = 8 ones
   2 tens × 4 = 8 tens
   $\begin{array}{r} 22 \\ \times\ 4 \\ \hline 88 \end{array}$

2. 1 one × 3 = 3 ones
   3 tens × 3 = 9 tens
   $\begin{array}{r} 31 \\ \times\ 3 \\ \hline 93 \end{array}$

3. 3 ones × 2 = 6 ones
   4 tens × 2 = 8 tens
   $\begin{array}{r} 43 \\ \times\ 2 \\ \hline 86 \end{array}$

4. 1 one × 6 = 6 ones
   1 ten × 6 = 6 tens
   $\begin{array}{r} 11 \\ \times\ 6 \\ \hline 66 \end{array}$

5. 1 one × 3 = 3 ones
   2 tens × 3 = 6 tens
   3 hundreds × 3 = 9 hundreds
   $\begin{array}{r} 321 \\ \times\ 3 \\ \hline 963 \end{array}$

6. 4 ones × 2 = 8 ones
   2 tens × 2 = 4 tens
   3 hundreds × 2 = 6 hundreds
   $\begin{array}{r} 324 \\ \times\ 2 \\ \hline 648 \end{array}$

7. 486
8. 488
9. 808
10. 550
11. 700
12. 909
13. 44 × 2 = 88
88 souvenirs are given away.
14. 21 × 4 = 84
Mrs. Raja uses 84 flowers.
15. 32 × 3 = 96
Allen prepares 96 sandwiches.
16. $204 × 2 = $408
Mrs. Tay pays $408 for the desks.

Lesson 7.3

1. Step 1 Multiply the ones by 4.
   6 ones × 4 = 24 ones
   Regroup the ones.
   24 ones = 2 tens 4 ones
   Step 2 Multiply the tens by 4.
   7 tens × 4 = 28 tens
   Add the tens.
   28 tens + 2 tens = 30 tens
   Regroup the tens.
   30 tens = 3 hundreds 0 tens
   Step 3 Multiply the hundreds by 4.
   1 hundred × 4 = 4 hundreds
   Add the hundreds.
   4 hundreds + 3 hundreds
   = 7 hundreds
   So, 176 × 4 = 704

2. Step 1 Multiply the ones by 3.
   5 ones × 3 = 15 ones
   Regroup the ones.
   15 ones = 1 ten 5 ones
   Step 2 Multiply the tens by 3.
   4 tens × 3 = 12 tens
   Add the tens.
   12 tens + 1 ten = 13 tens
   Regroup the tens.
   13 tens = 1 hundred 3 tens
   Step 3 Multiply the hundreds by 3.
   2 hundreds × 3 = 6 hundreds
   Add the hundreds.
   6 hundreds + 1 hundred
   = 7 hundreds
   So, 245 × 3 = 735

3. Step 1 Multiply the ones by 4.
   7 ones × 4 = 28 ones
   Regroup the ones.
   28 ones = 2 tens 8 ones
   Step 2 Multiply the tens by 4.
   4 tens × 4 = 16 tens
   Add the tens.
   16 tens + 2 tens = 18 tens
   Regroup the tens.
   18 tens = 1 hundred 8 tens
   Step 3 Multiply the hundreds by 4.
   1 hundred × 4 = 4 hundreds
   Add the hundreds.
   4 hundreds + 1 hundred
   = 5 hundreds
   So, 147 × 4 = 588

4. 716
5. 835
6. 938
7. 912
8. 998
9. 940
10. 538
11. 716
12. 984
13. 635
14. 882
15. 925
16. $285 × 3 = $855
    Gigi will save $855 in three years.
17. 458 × 2 = 916
    Jessie imports 916 roses in two months.
18. 164 × 6 = 984
    Rafi bakes 984 snacks in 6 days.

Put on your Thinking Cap!

1. a.
   ```
         1 6
       ×   7
       -----
       1 1 2
   ```
   b.
   ```
         2 8
       ×   4
       -----
       1 1 2
   ```
   c.
   ```
         5 6
       ×   2
       -----
       1 1 2
   ```

2. a.
   ```
         1 7
       ×   8
       -----
       1 3 6
   ```
   b.
   ```
         3 4
       ×   4
       -----
       1 3 6
   ```
   c.
   ```
         6 8
       ×   2
       -----
       1 3 6
   ```

3. Strategy: Make a list
   a. Possible 3-digit numbers
      (each digit is used only once):
      568, 586, 658, 685, 856, 865
      There are 6 three-digit numbers.
   b. Possible 3-digit numbers
      (each digit can be used more than once)

555	666	888
556	665	855
565	656	866
558	668	856
585	686	865
566	655	885
588	688	886
568	685	858
586	658	868

   $9 \times 3 = 27$
   There are 27 3-digit numbers.

4. a. 6 5 4
       ×   8

       5, 2 3 2

   b. 5 6 8
       ×   4

       2, 2 7 2

Chapter 8

Lesson 8.1

1. 8; 8
2. 9; 9
3. 8; 8
4. 6; 6
5. 7; 7
6. 9; 9
7. 8; 8
8. 9; 9
9. 7; 7
10. 9; 9
11. 36; 4; 40
12. 8; 2; 200
13. 6
14. 60
15. 3
16. 30
17. 4
18. 40
19. 40
20. 60
21. 70
22. 80
23. 90
24. 80

Lesson 8.2

1. 23 ones ÷ 4 = 5 R 3
   Quotient = 5 ones
   Remainder = 3 ones
   Each child has 5 stickers.
   There are 3 stickers left over.

2. 26 ones ÷ 6 = 4 R 2
   Quotient = 4 ones
   Remainder = 2 ones
   Each friend has 4 pizza slices.
   There are 2 pizza slices left over.

3. 4 R 7
4. 8 R 3
5. 6 R 5
6. 8 R 4
7. 8 R 4
8. 7 R 7
9. 10 R 3
10. 8 R 2
11. 9 R 1
12. 7 R 4

Lesson 8.3

1.
a.	b.
4,587	4,578
4,785	4,758
4,857	5,478
4,875	5,748
5,487	5,784
5,847	5,874
7,485	7,458
7,845	7,548
8,457	7,584
8,475	7,854
8,547	8,574
8,745	8,754

2. a. 7,603   b. 7,630
   c. 3,067   d. 3,076
3. a. 95   b. 40
   c. 985   d. 984
   e. 405   f. 408
   g. 9,854   h. 4,085

Lesson 8.4

1. 21 (E)
2. 12 (N)
3. 34 (L)
4. 33 (I)
5. 22 (K)
6. 10 (H)
7. 32 (S)
8. 11 (T)

9. 43 (A) 10. 23 (P)
11. 41 (M) 12. 20 (J)

$\underset{(11)}{T}\ \underset{(10)}{H}\ \underset{(21)}{E}\ \underset{(32)}{S}\ \underset{(12)}{N}\ \underset{(43)}{A}\ \underset{(33)}{I}\ \underset{(34)}{L}$

13. $63 \div 3 = 21$
There are 21 snacks in each jar.
14. $80 \div 8 = 10$ chairs
There are 10 chairs in each row.

Lesson 8.5

1. 34 (C)   2. 29 (A)
3. 17 (O)   4. 14 (T)
5. 12 (D)   6. 13 (E)
7. 12 (D)   8. 19 (N)
9. 18 (S)   10. 16 (R)
11. 24 (G) 12. 29 (A)

$\underset{(12)}{D}\ \underset{(17)}{O}\ \underset{(24)}{G}\ \underset{(18)}{S}\ \ \underset{(34)}{C}\ \underset{(29)}{A}\ \underset{(19)}{N'}\ \underset{(14)}{T}$

$\underset{(16)}{R}\ \underset{(13)}{E}\ \underset{(29)}{A}\ \underset{(12)}{D}$!

13. $72 \div 3 = 24$
The grocer sells 24 plums in a day.
14. $64 \div 4 = 16$
There are 16 chairs in each circle.

Put on Your Thinking Cap!

1. Thinking Skill: Identifying patterns and relationships

Strategy: Use guess and check, Make a list
Numbers divisible by 5 end with 5 or 0.
Make a list of even numbers. Check whether it is divisible by 9.

Even numbers	Divisible by 9
310	✗
320	✗
330	✗
340	✗
350	✗
360	✓
370	✗
380	✗
390	✗

Sharon is thinking of the number 360.

2. Thinking Skill: Identifying patterns and relationships

Strategy: Use guess and check, Make a list
If Granny gives 6 stickers

Number of stickers given away	Number of stickers left	Number of stickers at first
6	5	11
12	5	17
18	5	23
24	5	29
30	5	35
36	5	41
42	5	47

If Granny gives 7 stickers

Number of stickers given away	Number of stickers needed	Number of stickers at first
7	2	5
14	2	12
21	2	19
28	2	26
35	2	33
42	2	40
49	2	47

a. Granny has 47 stickers.
b. $42 \div 6 = 7$
$49 \div 7 = 7$
Granny has 7 grandchildren.

3. Strategy: Make a list
List 2-digit odd numbers between 50 and 100 that can be divided by 7:
56, 63, 77, 91
The difference between the digits is 3.
$6 - 3 = 3$
The number is 63.

4. Strategy: Make a list
List 2-digit odd numbers that are less than 50 and can be divided by 5 exactly:
15, 25, 35, 45
The sum of the digits is 9.
$4 + 5 = 9$
The number is 45.

Chapter 9

Lesson 9.1

1. 450 × 4 = 1,800
   There are 1,800 seats on a train.

2.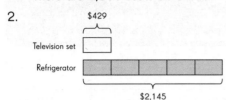

   $429 × 5 = $2,145
   The cost of the refrigerator is $2,145.

3.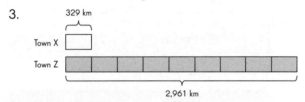

   329 × 9 = 2,961
   Town Z is 2,961 kilometers from Town Y.

4.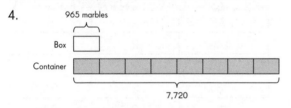

   965 × 8 = 7,720
   There are 7,720 marbles in the container.

Lesson 9.2

1.

   a. 457 × 3 = 1,371
      Rohani sold 1,371 tickets.
   b. 1,371 − 457 = 914
      Lilian sold 914 fewer tickets than Rohani.

2.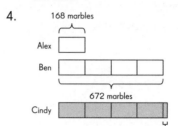

   27 × 3 = 81
   500 − 81 = 419
   They have 419 packets of seeds left.

3.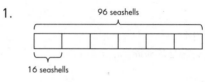

   68 × $7 = $476
   $476 + $46 = $522
   Mrs. Johnson paid $522 for the posts and the wire.

4.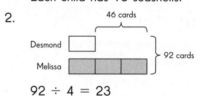

   a. 168 × 4 = 672
      Ben had 672 marbles.
   b. 672 + 28 = 700
      Cindy had 700 marbles.

Lesson 9.3

1.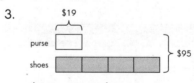

   96 ÷ 6 = 16
   Each child has 16 seashells.

2.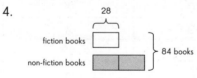

   92 ÷ 4 = 23
   23 × 2 = 46
   Desmond has 23 cards.

3.

   $95 ÷ 5 = $19
   Lynette pays $19 for the purse.

4.

   84 ÷ 3 = 28
   There are 28 fiction books on the bookshelf.

Lesson 9.4

1.

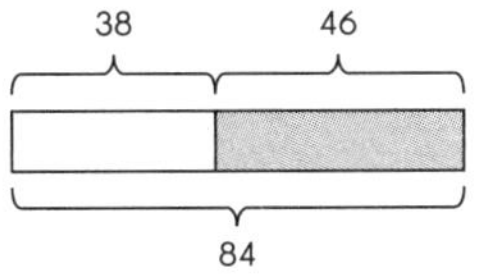

38 + 46 = 84

Sophia prepares 84 sandwiches in all.

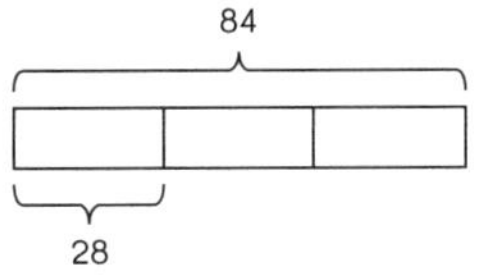

84 ÷ 3 = 28

Each platter has 28 sandwiches on it.

2. a.

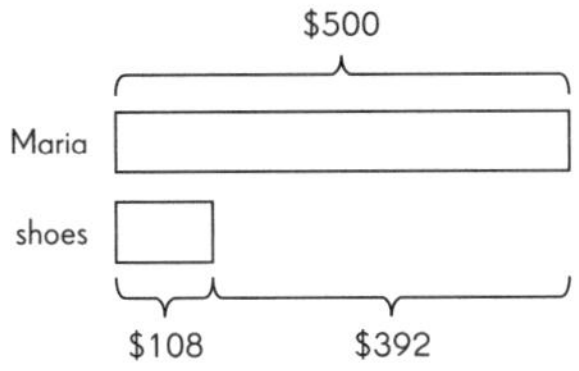

$500 − $108 = $392

Maria gives $392 to her 4 nieces.

b.

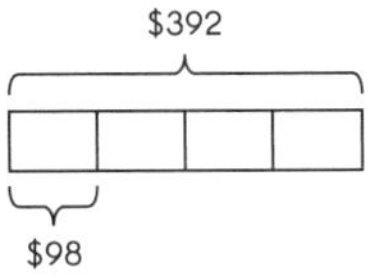

$392 ÷ 4 = $98

Each niece gets $98.

3.

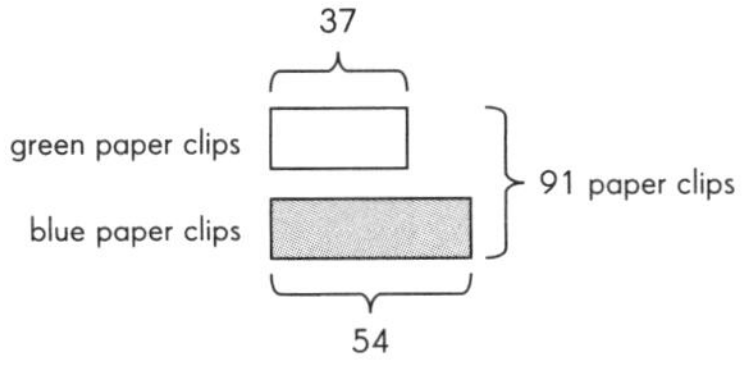

37 + 54 = 91

Corrine buys 91 paper clips.

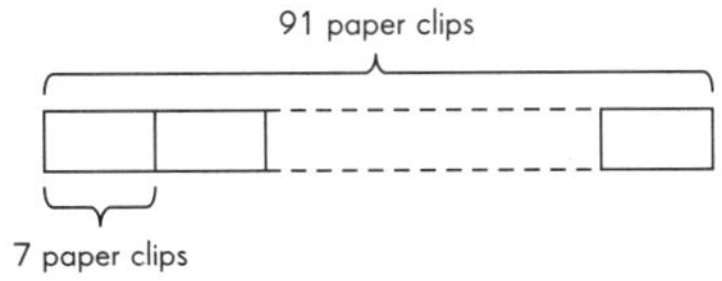

91 ÷ 7 = 13

There are 13 packets of paper clips.

4.

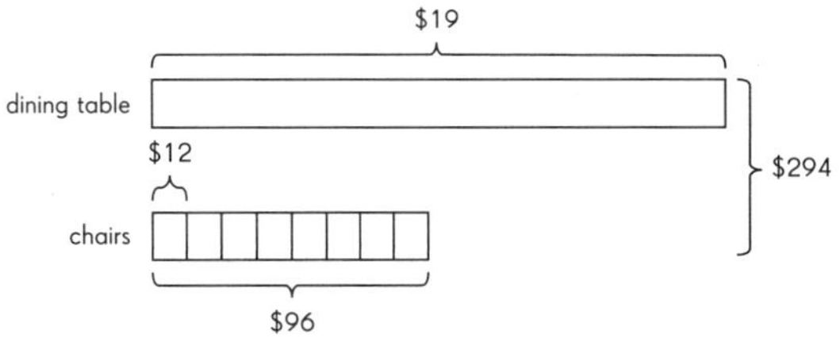

$294 − $198 = $96

$96 ÷ 8 = $12

Each chair costs $12.

5.

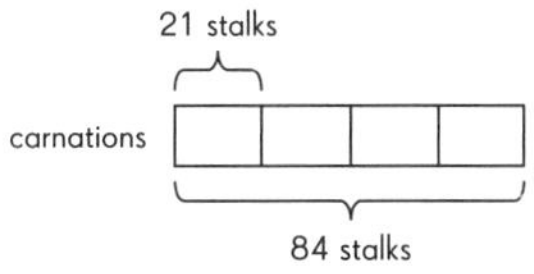

21 × 4 = 84

The florist buys 84 carnations.

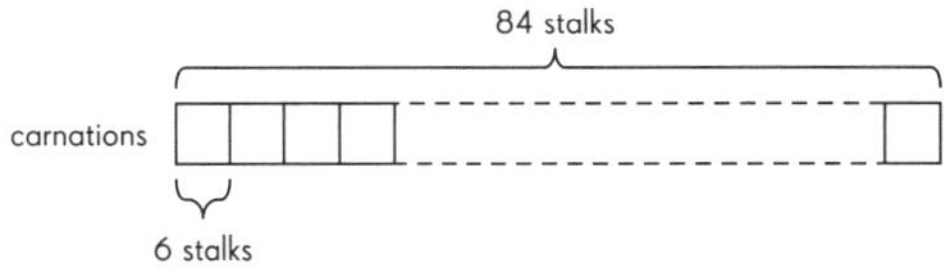

84 ÷ 6 = 14

There are 14 bouquets of carnations.

6.

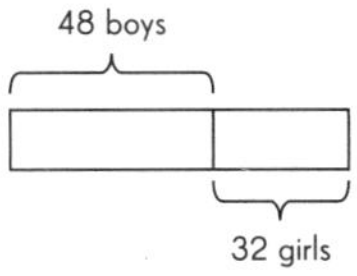

48 + 37 = 85

85 children take part in the competition.

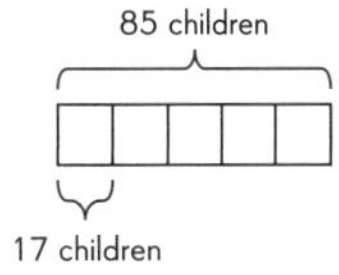

85 ÷ 5 = 17

There are 17 children on each team.

7.

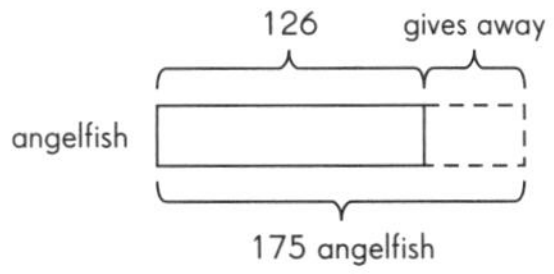

175 − 126 = 49

Clifford gives 49 angelfish to his friends.

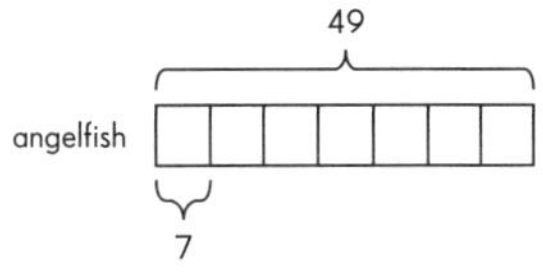

49 ÷ 7 = 7

Each friend gets 7 angelfish.

8.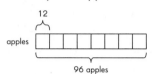
16 × 6 = 96
Adir buys 96 apples.

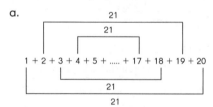
96 ÷ 8 = 12
There are 12 apples in each carton.

Put on Your Thinking Cap!

1. a. 180 + 90 = 270
    270 toys are sold in February.
    b. 270 × 3 = 810
    810 toys are sold in March.
    c. 810 − 320 = 490
    490 toys are sold in April.
    d. 180 + 270 + 810 + 490 = 1750
    1,750 toys are sold during the four months.

2. 135 − 37 = 98
    98 ÷ 2 = 49
    49 + 37 = 86
    Teresa makes 86 pins.

3. $8 × 3 = $24
    $5 − $3 = $2
    $2 → 1 day
    $24 → 12 days
    $5 × 12 = $60
    $60 + $8 = $68
    Each boy has $68 at first.

4. Thinking skill: Identifying patterns and relationships
    a.
    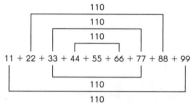
    There are 10 pairs of numbers.
    Each pair of numbers has a sum of 21.
    So,
    1 + 2 + 3 + 4 + 5 + ... + 17 + 18 + 19 + 20
    = 21 × 10
    = 210

    b.
    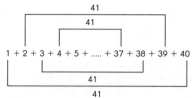
    There are 20 pairs of numbers.
    Each pair of numbers has a sum of 41.
    So,
    1 + 2 + 3 + 4 + 5 + ... + 37 + 38 + 39 + 40
    = 41 × 20
    = 820

    c.

    Each pair of numbers adds up to 110.
    So,
    11 + 22 + 33 + 44 + 55 + 66 + 77 + 88 + 99
    = 110 × 5 + 55
    = 550 + 55
    = 605

5. a. 2 or 5   b. 1, 3, 5, 7, or 9
    c. 0 or 5   d. 2, 5, or 8
    e. 2 or 6   f. 0, 2, 4, 6, or 8
    g. 8   h. 2, 4, 6, or 8
    i. 6   j. 1

Mid-Year Test Prep

1. B   2. C   3. D   4. C
5. D   6. C   7. C   8. D
9. D   10. B   11. D   12. B
13. D   14. D   15. D   16. D
17. A   18. B   19. A   20. C
21. 5,609   22. 700
23. 992   24. 13
25. 7,634   26. 4,571
27. 120   28. 620
29. 683   30. 14
31. 23   32. 676
33. 34, 55   34. 5,050
35. 47   36. 195
37. 47   38. 126

39. 28
40. 104
41. 148 + 65 = 213
    148 + 213 = 361
    The cafeteria sells 361 sandwiches and muffins.
42. 165 − 87 = 78
    78 ÷ 6 = 13
    Each neighbor receives 13 muffins.
43. 37 × 4 = 148
    Bobby has 148 books.
    148 − 69 = 79
    Clara has 79 books.
44. 96 ÷ 4 = 24
    The florist sells 24 lilies.
    24 + 78 = 102
    The florist sells 102 carnations.
45.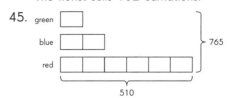
    765 ÷ 9 = 85
    85 × 6 = 510
    There are 510 red marbles in the box.

Extra Practice 3A 169

BLANK